Early Egypt

EARLY EGYPT

The Rise of Civilisation in the Nile Valley

A. J. SPENCER

University of Oklahoma Press
Norman

Oklahoma Paperbacks edition published 1995 by the University of Oklahoma Press, Norman, Publishing Division of the University, by special arrangement with British Museum Press, 46 Bloomsbury Street, London WC1B 3QQ

Library of Congress Cataloging-in-Publication Data
Spencer, A. Jeffrey.
    Early Egypt/the rise of civilisation in the Nile Valley/A.J. Spencer
      p. cm.
    Includes bibliographical references and index.
    ISBN 0-8061-2783-x (pbk.: alk. paper)
     1. Egypt—Civilisation—to 332 B.C.   I. Title.
DT61.S845   1995   95-17246
932—dc20   CIP

Designed by Behram Kapadia
Typeset in Monotype Photina by SPAN

Printed and bound by Arti Grafiche Milanesi S.p.A., Italy.

FRONT COVER Ivory figure of a king in the regalia of the jubilee festival. Probably First Dynasty, about 3100–2890 BC. From Abydos. H. 8.8 cm. (See also Fig. 52.)

BACK COVER The pyramid of Meidum, seen from the east. Fourth Dynasty, about 2600 BC.

FRONTISPIECE Ivory figurine of a woman, with inlaid eyes of lapis lazuli. Early Predynastic, fifth millennium BC. H. 11 cm.

Contents

Preface

The purpose of this book is to serve as an introduction to the formative stage of Egyptian civilisation, from earliest times through the Predynastic Period and early dynasties to the beginning of the Old Kingdom. This field is one in which many new discoveries have been made in recent years, and fresh material is still appearing from current excavations in Egypt. The modern evidence has been incorporated into this publication, and in particular I am most grateful to Dr Gunter Dreyer of the German Archaeological Institute in Cairo for permission to use photographs of his excavations at Abydos. For photographs of earlier discoveries I would like to thank the Egypt Exploration Society for allowing the use of images from the Society's archives.

In the preparation of the text I have benefited from discussions with my colleagues in the Department of Egyptian Antiquities of the British Museum; special thanks are due to Dr Stephen Quirke and Dr Richard Parkinson, who carried out the final proof checking and index preparation during my absence on excavation in Egypt. The editing of the volume was ably carried out by Teresa Francis of British Museum Press.

I am also grateful to Christine Barratt and Richard Parkinson for drawing the line illustrations, and to Peter Hayman of the British Museum Photographic Service for the majority of the photography.

Unless otherwise specified, all objects illustrated are in the British Museum.

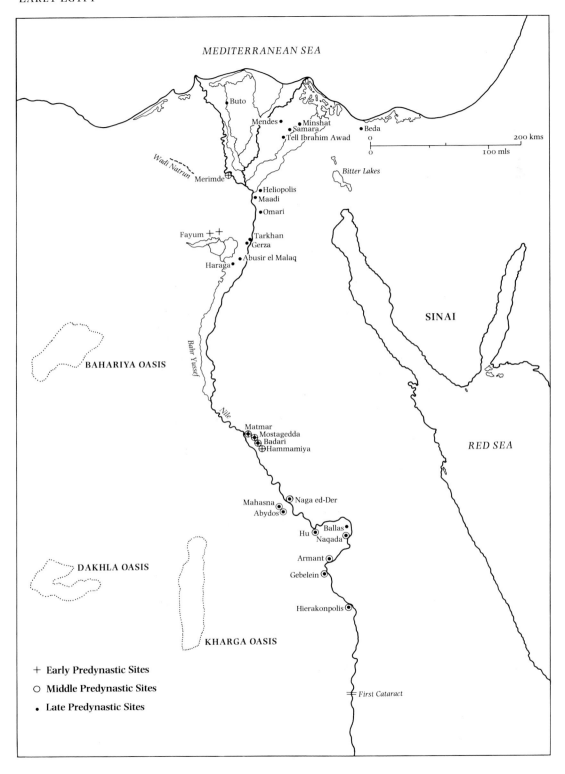

Introduction

The discovery of Predynastic Egypt

Before 1895, the history of Egypt was known only as far back as the reign of King Sneferu in around 2600 BC. In the first edition of his *History of Egypt*, published in 1894, Flinders Petrie wrote: 'The first three dynasties are a blank, so far as monuments are concerned; they are as purely on a literary basis as the kings of Rome or the primeval kings of Ireland.'

Ironically, it was Petrie who was to be the main agent responsible for filling this blank period with new information, the product of his own excavations in Egypt. The period from 1895 until 1900 was the most fruitful five years of fieldwork ever conducted for the illumination of the early history of Egypt, during which not only were monuments of the Early Dynastic kings discovered, but a long sequence of Predynastic remains also came to light.

In the winter of 1895, Petrie excavated at the site of Naqada in Upper Egypt, not far north of modern Luxor, and was rewarded with the discovery of vast cemeteries containing simple graves of unfamiliar type. The graves consisted of shallow pits in the desert, some with the refinement of mud-brick lining, containing bodies in a tightly contracted position and surrounded by pottery and objects of kinds not previously seen. This new discovery did not fit very well with what was already known of Egyptian burial customs of the Dynastic Period, but Petrie was initially reluctant to claim that the cemeteries should be assigned to a date prior to the First Dynasty. There seemed to be no suitable place in which the mass of new material could be assimilated into the mainstream of Egyptian history. Petrie's solution was to place the Naqada antiquities into the rather poorly documented period between the end of the Old Kingdom and the rise of the Middle Kingdom, that is between about 2200 and 2000 BC. Even in this position, the new objects did not look at all similar to other material of the period, and so it was proposed that they were products of a new race which had come into the Nile Valley. More graves of the same kind were found in the following year at Abydos, by Jacques de Morgan, who promptly guessed that they belonged to a prehistoric population, although he offered no supporting evidence. Confirmation of the true Predynastic age of the new discoveries had to wait for Petrie's own work of the 1898–9 season at the sites of Abadiya and Hu, not far north of Naqada, where more cemeteries of the same type were found.

The discovery of the Predynastic remains created a problem: it was quite evident that the mass of antiquities which had been excavated must

1 Map of Egypt, showing the principal sites associated with the various stages of Predynastic civilisation.

have been produced over a considerable span of time, but how was the material to be sorted into its correct chronological order? The archaeology of the later phases of Egyptian civilisation had the advantage of written records to provide dating evidence, but for the Predynastic cultures, which predated the emergence of writing, this tool was not available. The solution devised by Petrie has now become a standard archaeological technique, namely, placing the material in historical sequence without the luxury of fixed dates. For reference purposes, a set of numbers was chosen – which Petrie called 'Sequence Dates' – to which particular styles of object could be related. In his original system, Petrie assigned the numbers 30 to 80 to the Predynastic Period, leaving numbers 1 to 29 free for possible future discoveries. The ordering of the antiquities from the cemeteries involved a painstaking process of typological study, through which the relative frequency of occurrence of different styles of pottery in the graves was used to assemble the burials into groups. The Sequence Dating so devised was later found to require some modification, and Petrie adjusted the end of the Predynastic sequence from S.D. 80 to S.D. 76, a point deemed equivalent to the start of the First Dynasty. Subsequent research has shown that even this revised date was too high, and the beginning of the First Dynasty is now set at S.D. 63. The same relative dating procedure, or seriation, has recently been attempted with the aid of computers to analyse the Predynastic pottery from selected sites, with results which agree in most cases with those achieved by Petrie.

One of the problems with the study of Predynastic Egypt is the multiplication of alternative names for individual stages of development, brought about by the habit of naming cultures after the site of their discovery. As a consequence, the terms Amratian (after the site of El-Amra), Gerzean (from El-Gerza) and Semainian (from Es-Semaina) were chosen by Petrie to describe three stages of the Predynastic Period. It was later discovered that practically all the Semainian objects in fact belonged to the First Dynasty and so this term has been discarded. Another category found in old literature but now rarely used is 'Protodynastic', applied to remains from the period of the unification of Egypt and immediately after. Unfortunately, the names Amratian and Gerzean did not disappear but remained in use side by side with the alternative designations Naqada I and Naqada II, with which they overlapped. Generally speaking, the Amratian Period is the same as that now more commonly referred to as Naqada I and Gerzean is equivalent to Naqada II.

Some badly needed order was introduced following a major reassessment of the Predynastic Period in 1957 by the German scholar Werner Kaiser, who proposed a new system using the terms Naqada I, Naqada II and a new division, Naqada III. This has the advantage of indicating the continuity of the Naqada culture over time, and highlights the name of the site from which the culture spread. Within the three stages proposed by Kaiser are numerous subdivisions to illustrate more accurately the sequence of development of Predynastic goods. It is important to

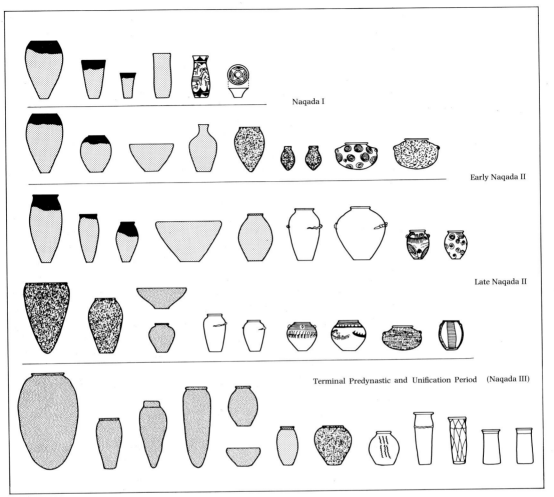

Naqada I

Early Naqada II

Late Naqada II

Terminal Predynastic and Unification Period   (Naqada III)

remember that there was always a certain amount of overlap between the individual phases as older traditions slowly died out and were replaced by new fashions.

The early years of the twentieth century, following the discovery of the Predynastic civilisations, saw a great deal of excavation in desert cemetery sites of Predynastic date. Many more burials of the Naqada people were discovered, particularly Naqada II graves in sites near the Fayum. A most important development was the discovery in the region of El-Badari in Upper Egypt of a culture earlier than that of Naqada, to which the name 'Badarian' was applied. This new phase was soon joined by others, with the excavation of equally early Predynastic remains at Merimde on the fringes of the Nile Delta, and around the Fayum depression. All these new discoveries included evidence of settlements as well as cemeteries, adding a new element to knowledge of the Predynastic Period. Sharp differences between the Predynastic finds made at Merimde in the north and those from the Upper Egyptian

2 Examples of Predynastic pottery styles, showing the changes which took place over time.

(southern) cultures became apparent, suggesting the existence of separate traditions in the two areas.

Recent archaeological investigation has produced new data on the spread of the Upper Egyptian Predynastic culture into the Delta region during the late Naqada II and Naqada III stages. Burials of this period have been found on the eastern side of the Delta, at the site of Minshat Abu Omar, accompanied by grave-goods of classic Naqada III style. The increasing pace of archaeological work in the Delta is beginning to reveal that Predynastic activity in the region was more widespread than had been supposed. Further work should help to clarify the nature of the Predynastic communities of Lower Egypt and is beginning to show how their lifestyle was steadily replaced by customs from the south.

Excavation and survey of Predynastic sites in Upper Egypt has continued to refine our knowledge of the Naqada culture, through the application of careful stratigraphic excavation techniques which can provide a better understanding of the great quantity of Predynastic antiquities previously recovered from cemeteries. Significant new finds have been made over the last twenty years at Hierakonpolis, a most important centre in both Predynastic and Early Dynastic times, and the remains of a Predynastic town at Naqada itself were investigated in the early 1980s by an Italian expedition. The relative dating of Predynastic remains – the method instigated by Petrie – has now been supplemented by the possibility of establishing fixed dates by the use of Carbon-14 or thermoluminescence dating techniques. One area which has not been neglected in recent years is the investigation of Egyptian prehistory, the time of the first hunter-gathering societies in the Nile Valley, extending back for some 200,000 years. At numerous sites, chiefly in Upper Egypt, evidence of early human activity has been recorded at different periods over a vast span of time.

Illuminating the early dynasties

The discovery of the Predynastic cultures occurred within a very few years of another significant step forward in Egyptology: the excavation at Abydos of the royal tombs of the First and Second Dynasties, the period previously described by Petrie as 'blank'. The tombs were first excavated by Emile Amélineau between 1894 and 1898, as part of a large-scale project which also included the clearance of some Predynastic graves, in addition to later monuments. The excavation could have been better supervised, even by the standards of the time, but nevertheless a mass of new material was discovered which shed light on the earliest kings of Egypt. The task of bringing the material into some kind of order was undertaken by Petrie, who was eventually permitted to excavate at Abydos after the departure of Amélineau. The tombs were dug again with greater attention to detail, and more objects, some of great importance, were found. Many items bore names of previously unknown kings, for which Petrie suggested a chronological sequence (see below, Chapter 4). One name from the group had already been encountered,

that of Narmer, known from the discovery at Hierakonpolis in 1898 of the great decorated palette with scenes of this king victorious over his enemies.

Despite the repeated excavation of the royal tombs at Abydos, more material remained to be discovered in work carried out since 1973 by the German Archaeological Institute. Detailed investigation of the architecture of the tombs revealed new information on their construction, including evidence for several stages of building. Additional inscribed objects were found and the links between the royal tombs and the nearby Predynastic cemetery were explored. At some distance from the tombs a separate expedition of Pennsylvania University Museum has discovered remains of boats buried under brickwork, which may be connected with the Early Dynastic tombs. These new finds remain to be investigated in

3 The tomb of King Den at Abydos, during excavation by Flinders Petrie in 1900. The entrance stairway into the burial chamber is at the rear.

13

detail, but it is interesting to note that wooden boats were buried beside certain First-Dynasty tombs at Saqqara, and, in the Old Kingdom, alongside some of the royal pyramids.

Although a large number of cemetery sites of the early dynasties have been found throughout Egypt as a result of early excavations, and more continue to be discovered in new fieldwork, one of the most informative is the site of Saqqara. The earliest tombs in this great necropolis of the ancient capital at Memphis date from the First Dynasty, and include a series of fine brick-built tombs of high officials, occupying the ridge along the eastern edge of the desert. The rectangular superstructures of such tombs have long been described by the Arabic term 'mastaba', meaning a bench, because of a similarity in shape to the mud-brick benches found outside traditional village houses in Egypt. These tombs were explored by Bryan Emery between 1936 and 1956 and from them came a wealth of information on the architecture, funerary practices and material culture of an élite stratum of First-Dynasty society. So fine was the burial equipment that Emery suggested that these were the tombs of the kings themselves, relegating the Abydos monuments to the role of symbolic cenotaphs, but this theory has not remained tenable. Also at Saqqara are a great number of tombs belonging to the Second and Third Dynasties, the excavation of which by J.E. Quibell in the years 1912–14 and C.M. Firth in 1930 helped to fill the gap in the archaeological record between the increasing number of First-Dynasty monuments and the beginning of the Old Kingdom. It is still true that we know less about the Second and Third Dynasties than we do about the First.

Although the majority of information about the early dynasties has been gained through excavation, some guidance was available from ancient written sources, thanks to the records left by the ancient Egyptians themselves about their own history. Lists of kings compiled in the New Kingdom and inscribed on the walls of temples or tombs, although primarily connected with a cult of the royal ancestors, nevertheless have considerable value for historical research. The monumental lists which include kings of the Early Dynastic Period are known as the Karnak, Saqqara and Abydos Lists, the last of which, located in the temple of Seti I, is the best preserved. There is also a papyrus version of a king-list on a famous but very fragmentary document in Turin, with the added value that the lengths of reign of the individual kings are included. An ancient historical document of a slightly different kind was compiled in the Fifth Dynasty, when the major events of the first five dynasties were inscribed on a slab of basalt. One piece from this valuable inscription is now in the Museum in Palermo, and is consequently known as the Palermo Stone, and other small fragments are kept in the Cairo Museum and the Petrie Museum in London, but the majority of the original slab is missing. The surviving parts include mention of the major political and religious events of the reigns of several kings of the First and Second Dynasties.

Documents like the Turin papyrus must have been used for the compilation of histories of Egypt, such as that written by Manetho, an

Egyptian historian of the third century BC, to whom we owe the framework of dynasties so conveniently used for the chronological ordering of events. Manetho's history suffers from errors of compilation from older sources and survives only in much later copies, adding to the confusion of details. The names of Early Dynastic rulers contained in the king-lists and Turin papyrus are also recorded by Manetho, but there are in some cases considerable differences between the spellings of the names in the various sources. This is the result of phonetic change, errors and confusion over the length of time involved between the Early Dynastic Period and the date at which the lists were compiled. The full royal titulary in Egypt eventually developed to include five separate names and it must be remembered that the lists give the so-called *nsw*-names of the kings rather than the Horus-names which were more frequently used in the First and Second Dynasties. As an example, the name of the First-Dynasty king with the Horus-name Den and *nsw*-name Semti appears in the Abydos list in the form Septi, through confusion of the hieroglyphs for Semti with similar signs of different reading. In the copies of Manetho's history the name was written in Greek in the form Usaphais, in which only a faint hint of the original version remains. Once the names of the

4 Part of the king-list in the temple of Seti I at Abydos, with the names of the First-Dynasty kings. Nineteenth Dynasty, about 1280 BC.

early kings began to be discovered on contemporary monuments found in excavation, however, it was possible to trace the link with the names given in the later sources in spite of their distorted forms. The fact that so many of the names actually agree is an indication of the quality of the ancient Egyptian records.

One of the most impressive features of the rise of civilisation in the Nile Valley is the acceleration of technical and social advance during the Early Dynastic Period. For over 150,000 years a Stone Age way of life had persisted in the Nile Valley, followed by about two millennia of Predynastic settlement, but the next four hundred years saw the emergence of a powerful, unified State, the construction of great monuments and the consolidation of the styles and symbols which were to remain characteristic of Ancient Egypt.

I

The Stone Age and the
Early Predynastic Cultures

Palaeolithic hunter-gathering peoples

Long before the construction of the great monuments for which
ancient Egypt is famous, the earliest hunter-gathering peoples
were active in the valley of the Nile. Evidence of their presence
remains in the form of the stone tools which they made, generally hand-
axes, roughly chipped to shape from cores of natural flint. The oldest
implements date from the mid-Pleistocene period, several hundred
thousand years ago, and occur in high-level gravel terraces on the desert
fringes of the valley. Primitive hand-axes have been found at Nag Ahmed
el-Khalifa, to the south of Abydos. The climate was not always so arid as
it is today and prolonged pluvial periods are known to have occurred,
during which many animal and plant species were able to flourish in
areas which have now become desert. From air photographs it is possible
to see the many ancient watercourses which twist through the high
plateau of Egypt's Eastern Desert, now reduced to dry channels. Some
desert regions were once forested, as shown by the presence of the
fossilised remains of trees.

   Middle Palaeolithic sites of between 100,000 and 50,000 BC have
yielded implements produced by the so-called Levallois technique,
through which flakes of desired shapes could be created. The sites at
which tools have been found seem to have been sources of flint, extracted
from the desert gravel by trenching. Far more elaborate flint mining
occurred at a period around 33,000 BC at the site of Nazlet Khater south
of Asyut. After cutting trenches in the gravel to reach the stratum of flint,
the miners proceeded to work underground, by tunnelling along the
flint-rich layer. The depth of the subterranean workings was in the
region of two metres. With the flint from these quarries, the inhabitants
produced much more advanced tools than the heavy hand-axes of the
early Palaeolithic period. Thin blades were struck from cores to prepare
implements for delicate work and the cutting edges of larger tools
were sometimes resharpened by careful flaking. Further advance is
represented by the fine retouched flake tools from the site of Shuwikhat,
near Qena, where there was a hunting and fishing camp from about
25,000 BC.

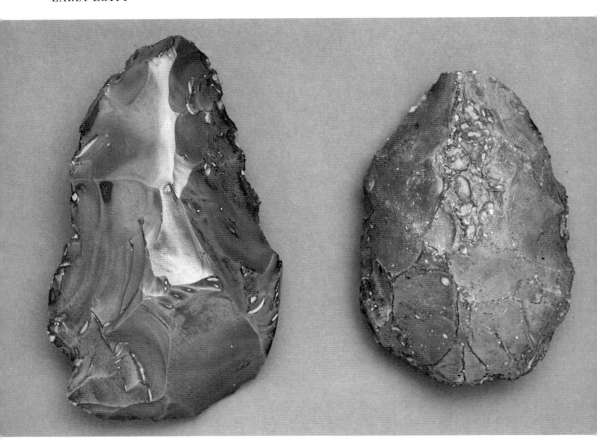

5 Two flint hand-axes, roughly chipped to shape from cores. Palaeolithic, before 100,000 BC. From Thebes. L. 16 and 13 cm.

Most sites of the Late Palaeolithic period, from 21,000 to 12,000 BC, are located in Upper Egypt, which at the time was subject to an extremely dry climate. At Kubbaniya near Esna a seasonal lake afforded opportunities for fishing on an intermittent basis in around 20,000 BC. Some 8,000 years later, a community at Makhdama near Qena was also combining fishing and hunting, and the considerable numbers of fish bones recovered show the importance of fish in the diet. It has been suggested that the large quantities of carbon found at the site are the remains of fires used for drying fish. Between about 11,000 and 8,000 BC there is an apparent gap in the evidence for human activity in the Nile Valley, unless the remains of the age have been completely covered by alluvial deposits. Traces of human presence reappear at the end of this interval at a time of increased rainfall. The lifestyle of the people remained truly Palaeolithic, with hunting and fishing carried out from seasonal camps.

6 Map of the principal Palaeolithic sites in Egypt.

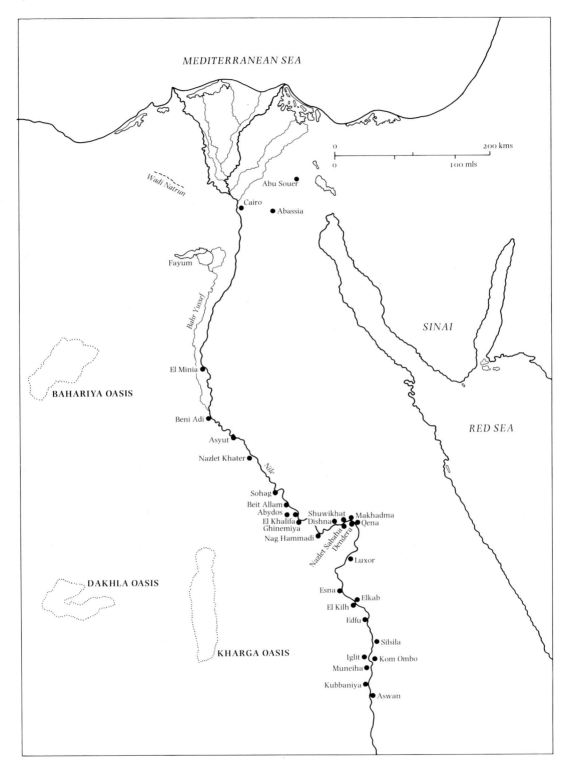

MEDITERRANEAN SEA

Wadi Natrun

Abu Souer

Cairo
Abassia

0
200 kms
0
100 mls

Fayum

Bahr Yussef

SINAI

BAHARIYA OASIS

El Minia

RED SEA

Beni Adi

Asyut

Nazlet Khater

Nile

Sohag
Beit Allam
Abydos
El Khalifa
Ghinemiya
Nag Hammadi

Shuwikhat
Dishna
Makhadma
Qena
Nazlet Sabaha
Dendera

Luxor

DAKHLA OASIS

Esna

Elkab

El Kilh

Edfu

KHARGA OASIS

Silsila

Iglit
Muneiha

Kom Ombo

Kubbaniya

Aswan

Early Predynastic settlements in Lower Egypt

The development of agriculture may have been promoted by climate changes which began in about 7000 BC and which allowed many plant and animal species to flourish in the region of the present-day Sahara. Agricultural communities appeared in the late sixth millennium BC, the first of the so-called Predynastic cultures, which were essentially Neolithic communities, despite the fact that some of these early cultures possessed a very limited knowledge of copper. Some of the oldest remains have been found around the Fayum depression, where two phases of settlement, designated A and B by the excavator, have been identified. A re-evaluation of the evidence has shown, contrary to the excavator's view, that the Fayum B stage was the earlier of the two and should be regarded as belonging to the last stage of the Palaeolithic period, prior to 6000 BC. The succeeding Fayum A phase was a true Predynastic community, practising agriculture in addition to hunting from about 5000 BC. The appearance of these settlers was closely linked with climatic changes which brought about the gradual reflooding of the Fayum lake after a long period of desiccation. Shelter was available beside the sandstone outcrops around the lake depression and an abundance of game was available for hunting in addition to the fish in the lake. Suitable land for agriculture existed in the region, but animal domestication seems to have been very limited, perhaps because of the plentiful wildlife. The animals present around the lake included species which have long since disappeared from the area, such as gazelle, elephant, hippopotamus and crocodile.

The Fayum culture had a flourishing flint industry, producing fine arrowheads and sickle blades. The latter were fitted into handles of tamarisk wood to make efficient agricultural tools, the edges of the sickle blades sometimes exhibiting a distinct polish as a result of use. The grain cultivated in the Fayum was emmer wheat and barley, which was stored in silos formed from pits in the ground, lined with basketwork. The majority of the silos were around 1 metre in diameter and between 30 centimetres and 1 metre deep. Well-made baskets were used as portable containers, far more proficiently manufactured than the pottery of the Fayum culture, which consisted of coarse handmade vessels of highly utilitarian forms.

Some similarities have been noted between the products of the Fayum culture and those found at the site of Merimde, at the western edge of the Nile Delta, but the two communities may well have had distinct origins. The Predynastic remains at Merimde cover a very large area, and go back almost as early as the remains in the Fayum, to some period not long after 5000 BC, from which time a number of hearths and burials have survived. The inhabitants of this period probably built shelters of reeds, but at a later phase of occupation oval houses of wickerwork were constructed, also associated with numerous hearths. Still later, the dwellings were refined by the use of straw-tempered mud for the lower parts of the walls, with the interior floor level sunk into the ground by

7 Reed basket for the storage of grain. Early Predynastic (Fayum culture), about 5000 BC. L. 52 cm.

about 40 centimetres. The difference in level beween the inside and outside created a need for a step, which in many cases was formed from the tibia of a hippopotamus. In the latest phase of the settlement the houses were distributed along a primitive, winding street, as the urban nature of the settlement developed. The burial of the dead in the village area rather than in a separate cemetery may indicate differences from the usual practice of the contemporary Upper Egyptian Predynastic cultures, provided that the burials at Merimde were made within the occupied settlement and were not subsequent intrusions in abandoned areas. A lack of grave-goods with the burials at Merimde is a more important departure from the usual practice further south.

In common with the Predynastic settlers of the Fayum, the pottery produced by the inhabitants of Merimde was plain and utilitarian, contrasting sharply with the polished ceramics of the Badarian and Naqada I peoples of Upper Egypt. Basketry was important, and was used for the lining of grain-pits as in the Fayum, and there was a developed industry in stone implements. The mixed economy included both agriculture and hunting, and pigs, cattle, sheep and goats may have been reared.

The evidence from the Fayum and Merimde shows the early Predynastic communities in the northern part of the Nile Valley to have been quite distinct from those of Upper Egypt, the Badarian and Naqada civilisations. The Lower Egyptian Predynastic settlers had more in common with the eastern Mediterranean than with the population of Upper Egypt, a difference which may explain the later Egyptian tradition of separate kingdoms of the north and south.

The separate identity of Lower Egypt has also been revealed by excavations at the site of El-Omari, south of the apex of the Nile Delta, where there was a community related to that of Merimde, although of later date. The first occupation of El-Omari may have taken place soon after 4000 BC, contemporary with the Naqada I culture of Upper Egypt, and the site remained settled until the end of the Predynastic Period. The early remains consisted of circular huts with sunken floors, like those of Merimde. The floors were covered by reed matting, perhaps coated with clay. At first the dead were buried in the settlement area with few grave-goods, but later in the history of the site separate cemeteries developed. The nature of the El-Omari community fits the pattern of the northern Egyptian Predynastic sites which were to be absorbed by the culture of Upper Egypt, and it was the attitudes of the latter culture which conditioned the thinking of the Dynastic civilisation.

Upper Egyptian Predynastic cultures

The earliest of the Predynastic cultures of Upper Egypt is the Badarian, so called because it was first identified at the site of El-Badari near Asyut. Subsequently, Badarian remains were found at a number of sites in the

8 Vase in the form of a hippopotamus, carved from elephant ivory. Early Predynastic, fifth millennium BC. From Mostagedda. H. 6.3 cm.

9 Figure of a woman, carved in hippopotamus ivory. Early Predynastic, about 5000 BC. From Badari. H. 14.3 cm.

10 Fragment of a pottery figure of a woman. Early Predynastic, fifth millennium BC. From Badari. H. 11 cm.

same region, including Matmar, Mostagedda and Hammamiya. The beginnings of the Badarian culture go back to about 5000 BC and perhaps even slightly earlier, making it largely contemporary with the Predynastic communities of the Fayum and Merimde in the north. In spite of this, the products of the Badarian people are more advanced than those of the Lower Egyptian sites, showing both technological superiority and more attention to quality and aesthetic considerations.

At the site of Hammamiya, a deep deposit of Badarian settlement remains was found in a context which showed that it was earlier in date than the first phase of the great Naqada culture, antiquities belonging to which were known prior to the discovery of the Badarian material. More traces of occupation were found on the spurs of the low desert in the same region, in addition to cemeteries containing oval graves with the body in the contracted position. The proximity of the desert to the river valley in Upper Egypt provided an obvious site for the burial of the dead, a location which continued to be exploited for the same purpose in later times. The settlement areas at Hammamiya were marked by what were essentially rubbish deposits, together with evidence for hearths and grain-pits lined with basketwork, but there was no trace of houses. Possibly the shelters were made of perishable materials which have not survived.

The occupation areas contained objects of domestic character, such as pottery, stone tools, bone piercers and remains of basketwork, but the range of Badarian products is better illustrated by material from the burials. Bodies might be enclosed in basketry or skins, and linen found with certain burials is apparently the remains of clothing, which seems to have included kilts, robes and some form of headgear. The orientation of the majority of bodies was with the head towards the south, facing west, an attitude which remained prevalent in the succeeding Naqada culture. Items of personal adornment were common, particularly strings of shells used for anklets, bracelets and necklaces. Elaborate girdles or belts were found with some of the male burials, consisting of multiple strings of blue-glazed steatite beads. The early achievement of applying glaze to stone seems to have been an attempt to copy the appearance of turquoise, and glazed steatite was to remain a favourite material for small objects in later periods. Ivory and bone were used extensively for small objects such as beads, piercers, pins and needles and combs. The needles found in a few graves were true sewing implements, with remains of linen thread still present in the eye. They might be kept safely in bone cases of cylindrical shape. Ivory or bone was also used for the modelling of human and animal figures, one of the best examples of this work being a figurine of a woman carved from the lower canine of a hippopotamus. This figure was found in a grave at Badari and is now in the British Museum. Pottery could be used as an alternative to bone, and a fragmentary female figure in red pottery is in the same collection. Figures of animals were sometimes included in the embellishment of objects of daily use, such as a pottery bowl with small hippopotamus figures modelled around the rim or an ivory vessel carved entirely in the form of the same animal.

The Badarians used cosmetic materials for eye-paint, ground from mineral substances such as malachite. The material was ground on special stone palettes, using a pebble to crush the mineral on the surface of the stone. Palettes of the period were most frequently of rectangular shape with a slight notch in each narrow end, made of compact metamudstone and worked to a thickness of around 5–6 millimetres. Some palettes are stained green from the cosmetic prepared upon them, providing a clear confirmation of their use. A few palettes of different materials are known, such as calcite, but the grey mudstone was a favourite which remained popular for palettes in the succeeding Naqada culture.

One of the finest products of the Badarian culture was the pottery, which can easily be distinguished from that of the later stages of Predynastic Egyptian civilisation. All the pottery was hand-made, but nevertheless was worked into vessels, chiefly bowls, which were both

useful and attractive. The finest pottery was of red-brown colour with a blackened area around the rim, polished by burnishing with a pebble. The exterior of the vessel was often decorated with a pattern of very shallow grooves, apparently created by the use of some kind of comb-like tool. More utilitarian vessels were manufactured entirely in red-brown ware. The value of pottery is shown by the number of vessels with evidence of repair after breakage. This was achieved by drilling holes on either side of a break or crack, so that the edges could be drawn together tightly by binding, probably using strips of leather threaded through the holes. On the basis of certain forms of pottery, Guy Brunton suggested the existence of an earlier culture than the Badarian, which he named Tasian after the locality of Deir Tasa in Upper Egypt, but this view has not found general acceptance.

11 Polished pottery vase with the textured surface typical of the Badarian culture. Fifth millennium BC. From Badari. H. 22.8 cm.

The flintwork of the Badarians was relatively crude and relied on the rough working of nodules of chert rather than the use of mined material of better quality. The fine arrowheads and sickle blades present in Badarian graves may have been acquired from other areas of the Nile Valley or surrounding regions, where such items had a wide distribution.

The Naqada culture

There is no apparent break in the history of early Predynastic settlement in Upper Egypt between the end of the Badarian period and the beginning of the Naqada culture, and some authorities have suggested that there may have been an overlap between the two. That the Naqada culture continued long after characteristic Badarian products disappear is, however, beyond doubt, and the general sequence of the cultures was established by Caton-Thompson's stratigraphic excavations at Hammamiya.

The site of Naqada is located on the west bank of the Nile, about 50 miles north of the modern town of Luxor, and there is no doubt that it was the centre from which the Naqada culture expanded. Since its discovery, the Naqada civilisation has been the subject of much research, and the different stages through which it developed have been analysed and subdivided, as described in the Introduction to this book. For the purposes of general description, the terms used here have been restricted to the main phases of the culture, known as Naqada I, Naqada II and Naqada III, in order to avoid excessive detail inappropriate to a general work. The Naqada civilisation of Upper Egypt was the most important of all the Predynastic cultures, developing through its various stages to become dominant throughout the land.

The early stage, Naqada I, began in around 4000 BC and has left remains at sites throughout Upper Egypt as far north as Asyut. The majority of the sites which have been excavated have been cemeteries, many of which were also used during the later phases of the Naqada culture. The custom of burying objects in graves with the dead, already established by the Badarian people, was continued and expanded. The graves themselves were not too different from those of earlier times,

12 Cosmetic palettes in geometric and animal shapes. Predynastic (Naqada I culture), about 4000–3600 BC. w. of tortoise palette 20.3 cm.

consisting of shallow pits in the low desert, roofed with rough branches which may have supported a small tumulus of gravel. The bodies were placed in the usual contracted position, on the left side with the head to the south as in Badarian graves, but the objects buried with them included some items which were quite distinct from Badarian material. New types of pottery appeared, common among which was a highly polished red ware used for open bowls and tall, narrow vases. Some exotic shapes were also produced in this fabric, including vases with rounded, flattened bodies and a curious style of double vessel. In rare examples the red polished pottery was decorated with white-painted patterns, chiefly abstract geometric designs, but with occasional animal figures. The animals depicted include domesticated species like the goat but also wild creatures such as hippopotami, common in Egypt during the Predynastic Period.

The most common form of pottery introduced in the Naqada I period was the so-called black-topped ware, actually vessels with a red exterior but with the region around the rim polished black. This style had been used in Badarian times, although the colour and surface treatment of the vessels was different from those of Naqada I. Once established, the black-topped pottery continued in use until the end of the Naqada II period and is probably one of the most characteristic of all Predynastic products. The black top was probably created by inverting the vessel in the ash of a fire, where it would be subjected to heat with limited oxygen, so reducing some of the red iron oxide in the clay to the less oxidised black version.

The mudstone cosmetic palettes used by the Badarian people appear in new shapes during the Naqada I period, the most frequent of which was an elongated rhomboid. This shape is particularly interesting because in later times it became a symbol associated with the god Min, and served as the hieroglyph for the name of the god. Whether palettes of this shape had any special significance during the early Predynastic Period is difficult to say, but it is worth noting that some examples were made in

13 Bone comb with a figure of an animal carved on the top. Predynastic (Naqada I culture), about 4000–3600 BC. From Matmar. H. 12.5 cm.

14 Pottery vase
decorated with white
geometric patterns.
Predynastic (Naqada I
culture), about 4000–
3600 BC. H. 20.4 cm.

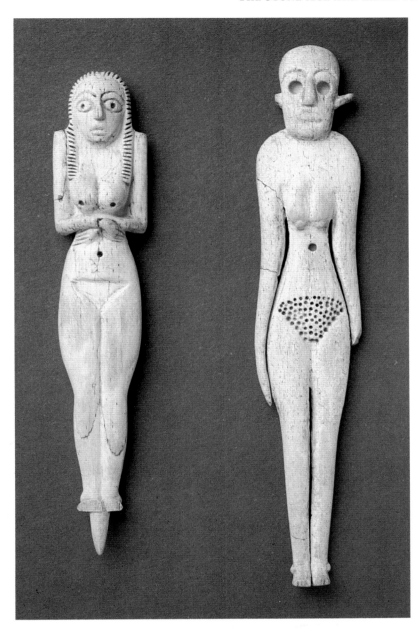

15 Two bone figurines of women. The right-hand figure was probably originally fitted with inlaid eyes of shell. Predynastic (Naqada I culture), about 4000–3600 BC. H. 10.6 and 12 cm.

very large sizes, not very convenient for their original purpose as a grinding surface. A possible magico-religious function for these objects is also hinted at by the adoption of palettes in the shapes of animals, particularly fish, turtles, hippopotami and antelope. In some examples the eyes of the animal were inlaid with shell.

Stone was used in the Naqada I period for vases, typically with two pierced lug-handles near the top of the sides to allow for the attachment of a cord. The preferred stone for these vases was basalt, a curious choice

16 ABOVE LEFT Carved bone tag in the shape of a tusk, the precise significance of which is unclear. Predynastic (Naqada I culture), about 4000–3600 BC. L. 9.5 cm.

17 ABOVE RIGHT Simple carved bone tag of a straight form, thought to be derived from a greatly abbreviated human figure. Predynastic (Naqada I culture), about 4000–3600 BC. From Matmar. L. 5.9 cm.

given the difficulty of working such a hard material. The interiors of the vessels show marks of rotary drilling, indicating that the crank drill with a stone bit, regularly used in later periods, had already been developed. Small cylindrical vases of softer materials, such as limestone, also occur in Naqada I period graves. The production of stone vases was to develop into a major industry in the Early Dynastic Period, to supply the demand for funerary equipment. Tools and weapons of the Naqada I culture also depended heavily on stone as raw material, although bone, ivory and a limited amount of copper were available as alternatives. Good-quality flint was mined for the production of effective cutting, scraping and piercing tools, but hard stones were used for making mace-heads. The latter objects occur in a disc-shape which is characteristic of the Naqada I period, but many of the examples do not seem to have been functional weapons. Some are of insufficient size and weight, and the perforation through the object for the handle is often so narrow as to prevent a blow being struck with any force without breaking the handle from the head. Just why so many of the mace-heads were ineffective is unclear, unless they are early examples of model substitutes for functional items in tomb equipment. Support for this view is provided by the finding of a painted pottery model of a disc-mace in a grave at Mostagedda. Two maces still attached to their original handles were found by Petrie in grave B86 at Abadiya, the handles being made of ivory and horn.

The bone and ivory carving of the Naqada I period includes pins and combs, frequently embellished with figures of animals, also rudimentary figurines, decorated tusks and so-called 'tags', flat strips of bone with incised surface decoration in the form of fine lines. The finest carved tusks have a human head at the top, but the significance of these objects is not known. Their use continued into the early part of the Naqada II period. The tags existed in two styles, one straight and the other slightly curved in imitation of tusks. It has been suggested that the straight examples had a different origin as highly abbreviated versions of human figures, some of which were made of flat strips of bone with almost no modelling apart from a rather triangular-shaped head at the top. Such figures seem to belong to an individual group, since other bone and ivory figurines made during the Naqada I period were considerably more detailed. The majority of these figures represent women, although a very fine example of a male figure was excavated at Mahasna.

The culture of the Naqada I period was firmly rooted in the Predynastic tradition of the southern part of the Nile Valley, with many similarities to the customs of the earlier Badarian population. Both of these cultures were products of the south and seem to have been remote from the Mediterranean world, although trade contacts with other lands were established through the desert and across the Red Sea. Throughout the early part of the Egyptian Predynastic Period, development was steady but not dramatic, as the fabric of society became more organised and the urban character of the major settlements increased. Had the same relatively slow rate of progress been maintained, it is unlikely that a politically unified Egyptian state would have come into existence in about 3100 BC; the move towards unification came with the appearance of the second stage of the Naqada culture, apparently spurred into more rapid innovation by the arrival of outside influences and new ideas.

2

The Later Predynastic Period

The emergence of the distinctive new products of the Naqada II stage of Upper Egyptian Predynastic civilisation has been seen as evidence of the arrival of a new people in the Nile Valley, who brought with them their own traditions. This does not mean that a great invasion took place; more probably there was a gradual and peaceful infiltration of newcomers, who seem to have been assimilated very easily into the existing population. Some continuity with earlier stages of Predynastic development is shown by the presence of traditional items, such as the black-topped style of pottery, in graves of Naqada II date, side by side with new types of funerary equipment. Although absolute dates are difficult to establish, it would seem from certain Carbon-14 measurements that the new phase began in around 3600 BC. The cultural tradition of Upper Egypt continued its advance to the north from the region of Asyut, and by late in the Naqada II period it had reached the settlements of the Nile Delta, such as Buto. The individual character of the Lower Egyptian Predynastic communities seems to have been gradually submerged by the spread of products from the south, long before the stage of any political union was reached.

The later Predynastic Period was a time of increasing urbanisation, as the settlement centres of Upper Egypt, such as Hierakonpolis and Naqada

18 Pottery model of a house with a timber-framed door indicated. At the opposite end are two windows, which must also have been framed with wood. Late Predynastic, about 3200 BC. From El-Amra. H. 23 cm.

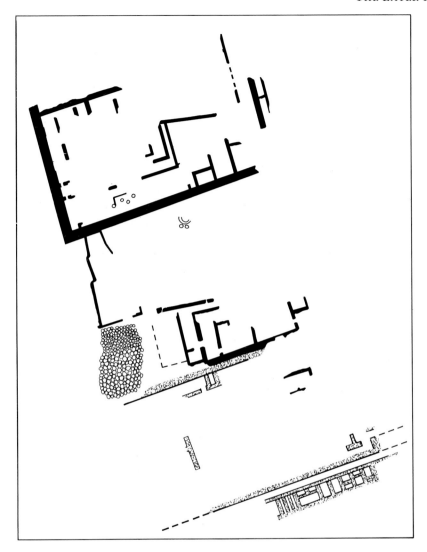

19 Plan of Predynastic buildings in the town excavated by Flinders Petrie at Naqada, one of the earliest urban settlements in the Nile Valley.

itself, expanded into large towns with a considerable use of mud-brick architecture. The town-site of Elephantine has also yielded remains of Naqada II date. Petrie excavated in the town at Naqada, and recorded the existence of rectangular buildings inside a perimeter wall, but unfortunately no good sequence of occupation levels was established comparable with the data retrieved from the cemeteries. A recent re-examination of the Predynastic town at Naqada by Italian archaeologists showed that the site has suffered severely from erosion since Petrie's day, so that the regular buildings which he excavated have been reduced to piles of fallen bricks. It was, however, possible to confirm that the town had existed throughout the various phases of the Naqada culture. Pre-dynastic remains at Hierakonpolis have been found in the desert west of the Nile and also on the site of the later city, situated in the river floodplain. The fact that rectangular brick houses were replacing the earlier fashion for circular huts during the Late Predynastic Period is shown by a pottery model of a house from a grave at El-Amra, near Abydos. This model is a representation of a house with squared angles and battered walls, in which are shown a door and two small windows, covered by what are surely wooden lintels. The grave from which it came also contained a pottery vase from the middle of the Naqada II period. Houses similar in appearance to this model can still be seen in rural communities in Egypt, although their number is decreasing very rapidly as fired brick and concrete replaces mud brick and mud plaster. Interestingly, some of the best examples of village houses resembling the model are located in the vicinity of Abydos.

The cemeteries of Naqada II followed the familiar Predynastic tradition of contracted burial, but the preparation of the grave shows some refinement, with a greater use of brick lining than previously encountered, probably a reflection of increasing wealth. Graves of rectangular as opposed to oval shape become more common, a development perhaps

20 Painted decoration from the tomb of an Upper Egyptian ruler at Hierakonpolis, showing boats, animals and human figures. Predynastic (Naqada II culture), about 3300 BC.

linked to the adoption of rectangular brick-built houses. The identification of burials of Naqada II date is most easily carried out on the basis
of the pottery, since it is the most common of the grave-goods and
because of the appearance of distinctive new forms. The red polished
vessels of Naqada I persisted for some time, including some of the white-
painted bowls, but a new class of rounded vases in a pink marl fabric
developed. These vases were often decorated in red paint, at first with
mottled or spiral patterns, but slightly later with complex scenes showing
boats, people, plants and animals. The abstract patterns seem to have
been intended to reproduce the appearance of vessels made from exotic
hard stones like breccia. Multiple wavy lines, probably an indication of
water, are also common in the decoration.

The decorated pottery of Naqada II has been the subject of much
discussion, in part because the stylised representations leave room for
various interpretations. At one time there was some controversy over
whether the objects shown on the pots were really boats or rather
schematic drawings of walled villages, but they are now generally

accepted as boats. This is clear evidence for the extensive use of timber, a material which was soon to appear in graves for the lining of the burial-pit. The boats are shown on the pottery with many oars and some type of cabin, frequently accompanied by some kind of emblem resembling the later standards of individual districts. Occasionally, human figures are depicted above the cabins on the boats, including a dancing woman with her arms raised, attended by male figures shown on a smaller scale. The female dancer seems to have possessed some significance in Predynastic mythology, and three-dimensional figurines of women in the same attitude as shown on the pots are known from graves of the Naqada II period. Unfortunately, very few of these figures, which were modelled in pottery, have been found in controlled excavations and a large number of forgeries exist in public and private collections. The figures are normally shown with the lower body and legs reduced to a single peg-like mass of clay and the features drastically abbreviated; sometimes the head resembles that of a bird rather than a human being. Their purpose in the graves is not known, although it has been suggested that they represented a goddess, or that they may have been connected with fertility and resurrection. The excavated figures came from burials which seem to be slightly earlier in date than the decorated pottery, suggesting that an existing belief found a new medium for expression in the painted ceramics.

Linked to the decoration of the Naqada II pottery are the remarkable paintings on the walls of the famous tomb 100 at Hierakonpolis, often referred to as the 'Painted Tomb'. Among the motifs included in the paintings are boats like the ones shown on the pottery, although curiously they lack the usual mass of oars. Numerous wild animals are depicted, interspersed with figures of men, some of whom are fighting amongst themselves whilst one appears to hold three captives. A tomb

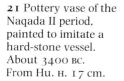

21 Pottery vase of the Naqada II period, painted to imitate a hard-stone vessel. About 3400 BC. From Hu. H. 17 cm.

22 Pottery vase of the Naqada II culture, with elaborate painted decoration consisting of scenes showing boats, animals and human figures. Among the latter is a dancing woman with her arms raised above her head. Predynastic, about 3500 BC. From El-Amra. H. 29.2 cm.

with such elaborate decoration must have belonged to an individual of great importance, possibly one of the local rulers who dwelt in Hierakonpolis in the Late Predynastic Period. Unfortunately, the tomb was not found intact when excavated in 1899 and the finest objects had already been removed, so the quality of the tomb equipment could not be assessed. Some of the pottery remained, with two stone vases and some flints, a collection which indicates a late Naqada II date for the tomb. The importance of the tomb is also reflected in its architecture, the walls and floor being formed of brick, a forerunner of the substantial brick-lined tombs of the early dynasties. There was even a cross-wall in the Hierakonpolis tomb to subdivide the pit, a feature which became common at the beginning of the First Dynasty, when it was used to separate the burial from some of the stored grave-goods.

To return to the pottery styles of the Naqada II period, other changes to the earlier repertoire included the appearance of utilitarian vessels in a coarse brown fabric, concisely described by Petrie as 'rough ware'. This kind of pottery formed a fairly high proportion of the ceramics in the burials of the period, but began to decline in the terminal phase of the

23 The 'Painted Tomb' at Hierakonpolis, from an excavation photograph taken in 1899. This was the burial place of an Upper Egyptian chief of the Late Predynastic Period, about 3300 BC.

Naqada culture, referred to as Naqada III. At this stage it was gradually replaced by a new range of vessels in a hard, smooth marl clay, pale beige in colour and of considerably superior quality and durability. The introduction of this pottery was probably also responsible for the disappearance of the old black-topped variety at around the same time. This new fabric, to which Petrie gave the name 'late ware', stands at the beginning of a long tradition of Egyptian pottery in which functional practicality was valued over decoration. In the middle of the Naqada II period another important class of jars appears in Egypt, with characteristic ledge-handles of wavy form at the sides. This type of pottery was used by Petrie for his sequence dating of the Predynastic material, by assuming a progressive alteration in the form of the vases over time, from wide, shouldered vessels with distinct wavy handles to more cylindrical shapes in which the handles declined to a mere ridge of clay, and finally to a painted or incised line. This sequence was a little over-simplified, since it has since been shown that some of the shouldered vases of wide and narrow form were contemporary, but the late adoption of the cylindrical style is confirmed. The original inspiration for this kind of vase was derived from imported vessels of similar style from Syro-Palestine, which were copied locally. Cylindrical vases were occasionally painted with a network of red lines, but by the end of the Predynastic Period they were made with a plain cream slip in imitation of limestone jars. The pottery with elaborate decoration, described above, did not last beyond the end of the Naqada II period and such painted vessels as occur from Naqada III bear only simple lines or dots.

Naqada II graves contained many items which were familiar from earlier in the Predynastic Period, such as maces and palettes, but the shapes of the objects had changed from those of Naqada I date. Instead of the disc mace-head we find a pear-shaped version, in addition to some narrow, pointed examples. The former style may be an example of influence from Mesopotamia, where maces of the same shape were produced. Cosmetic palettes of the early rhomboidal shape survived into the early part of Naqada II, sometimes with the added decorative feature of an animal head or other device at one or both ends. These, together with the palettes in the forms of turtles, hippopotami or other exotic creatures, were soon replaced by a less varied range of shapes among which those based on fish and birds predominate. Some palettes occur in such small sizes that they can only be considered as models, and they may have served as amulets. A very characteristic form of Naqada II palette was shaped like a shield, with two birds' heads at the top, facing outwards. Towards the close of the Predynastic Period the range of palettes was reduced even further, to abbreviated fish-shapes and oval or rectangular versions, some with cross-hatched decorative borders. Interestingly, at the same time as the small palettes were declining, a series of very large ceremonial examples appeared, decorated with scenes in relief commemorating political events. These decorated palettes are discussed in the next chapter.

Stone vessels became increasingly common in the later Predynastic Period and were made in a greater variety of materials. The common basalt of Naqada I still occurred, particularly for tall tubular vases, but it was now accompanied by limestone, sandstone, granodiorite and red breccia. Many of the stone vase shapes were modelled on pottery forms, so we find the ledge-handles or perforated lug-handles of Naqada II pottery reproduced on the stone versions. Towards the close of the Predynastic Period, stone vases were occasionally made in the shapes of animals, such as birds or frogs. Such exotic pieces are unlikely to have been produced for everyday use and were probably intended for the tomb equipment of particularly wealthy or important persons. This tendency continued in the early dynasties, when special products were made for the royal tombs.

One of the greatest achievements of the Naqada II culture was the production of some of the finest flint knives ever made anywhere in the world. These are in a totally different class from the roughly flaked implements produced by the Badarians, and can almost be considered works of art, since it is unlikely that the finest of them were ever used for anything other than ostentatious show. The blades were prepared by obtaining a piece of good-quality flint of suitable size to be shaped by grinding to the form required. A flat edge was created at the back of the

24 Siltstone palette with two birds' heads at the top. Late Predynastic (Naqada II culture), about 3600–3200 BC. H. 25.3 cm.

25 Vessel of red breccia in the form of a frog, with tubular handles at the sides. Late Predynastic to early First Dynasty, about 3100 BC. H. 3.6 cm.

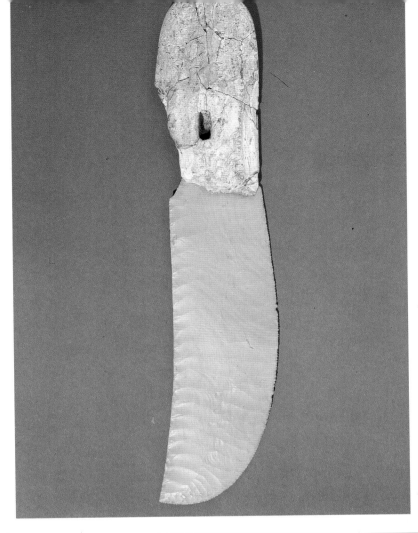

26 Flint knife with an ivory handle, on which are carved rows of animal figures including elephants, lions, oryx, Barbary sheep and oxen. The blade was shaped by grinding and pressure flaking. Late Predynastic, about 3200 BC. From Sheikh Hamada. L. 26.5 cm.

27 BELOW Pressure-flaked flint knives. Late Predynastic, about 3200 BC. L. 23.2 and 26.8 cm.

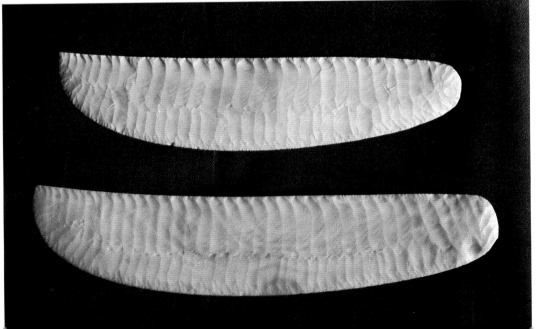

28 Basalt vase of tubular shape, with two small pierced handles for suspension. Late Predynastic (Naqada II culture), about 3600–3200 BC. H. 26 cm.

blade to provide a suitable surface from which small flakes of flint could be detached by pressure, a process done with such skill that each flake was of the same size and shape. This resulted in the creation of a rippled pattern along the length of the knife, but this pressure flaking was restricted to one face only, the other face being left as a smooth ground surface. Finally, the edge of the knife was worked into a series of very fine serrations. At the very end of the Predynastic Period such knives were sometimes fitted with carved handles of ivory.

The use of flint for small tools continued in Egypt far longer than is generally realised, and flake implements were still being produced in the fifth century AD, but at no time were the products so fine as in the Late Predynastic Period. Even in the First Dynasty a decline in quality had already set in; although some of the largest knives belong to this time, they were manufactured more rapidly by comparatively rough bifacial flaking. In addition to the decline in manufacturing technique, a clear alteration in the shape of flint knives can be traced from the Late Predynastic Period down to the Old Kingdom, which allows individual examples to be allocated to their correct period. The Late Predynastic knives are unmistakable; the fine ripple-flaking alone is sufficient to indicate their date. Their broad blades without handles are easily distinguished from First-Dynasty knives, which were made with an integral hook-shaped handle and a more pronounced concave curve to the back. By the late Second Dynasty this concave back was less obvious, the chipping of the tools had coarsened and the integral handles were losing the hook shape and becoming straight. Continued development into the early part of the Old Kingdom led to the production of knives with a straight or even slightly convex back, a short straight handle and the new feature of a pointed tip.

A curious use of flint in the Late Predynastic Period was the creation of figures of animals, or parts of animals, by chipping a flat piece of the stone to the necessary shape. These outline figures were not formed in any detail, since the material was unsuitable, but consisted of two-dimensional silhouettes chipped around the edges into the forms of birds, crocodiles, cattle and possibly dogs. The purpose of such objects is not known, but they probably had some amuletic value.

In the Naqada II period there was an increase in the use of metal, principally copper, although some silver is known from a grave near Nag Hammadi in Upper Egypt. This same burial is said to have contained a stone vase with gold-cased handles threaded with silver wire, an exotic object of a kind represented elsewhere from Early Dynastic contexts. Predynastic adzes of copper have been reported from Naqada and Abusir el-Melek and an axe of this metal was found at Matmar. It is not always easy to date these early metal objects from the limited information given on their archaeological context, but there is no doubt that some examples belong to the Naqada II period. Daggers of copper have been recovered from graves at El-Amra and Naqada, and from the former site a knife and a dagger of silver are reported, although these seem to belong to Naqada III. Valuable metals were used more regularly for small beads or thin wire, and a number of instances of the occurrence of gold and silver in Late Predynastic jewellery are known. A few iron beads from two graves at Gerza, near the Fayum, proved to be of meteoric origin.

The presence of gold or silver jewellery amongst the personal adornments of the dead is not always an indication of the richest graves. In describing the material from a tomb at Naqada, Elise Baumgartel commented on the contrast between the wealth implied by the presence of gold and the otherwise 'shabby contents' of the grave. The same contrast is illustrated by a burial group excavated at Abydos, from which came a fine diadem of gold, turquoise, garnet and malachite beads, now in the British Museum. The other material in the grave was mundane, consisting of pottery jars of late Naqada II types, including several of the

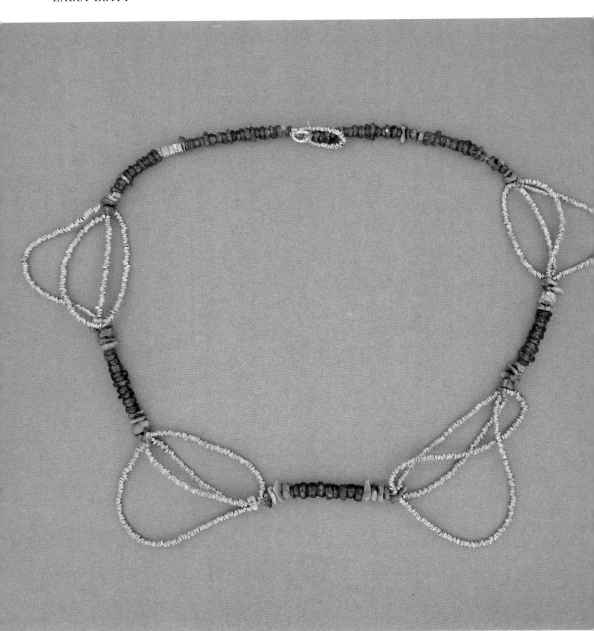

29 Diadem of gold, turquoise, garnet and malachite beads, found on the head of a female in a burial at Abydos. Late Predynastic, about 3250 BC. L. 31.2 cm.

common black-topped vessels, some rough ware vases and two small decorated pots. There was also an appallingly coarse flint knife, possibly intended as a model for funerary purposes only. Tomb-groups of this kind in ordinary Late Predynastic cemeteries show that some of the wealth of the élite class was gradually percolating throughout society, but also that individuals with only limited resources first acquired personal items such as jewellery, even if they could not obtain high-quality tomb equipment. This fits the pattern which evolved in later Egyptian funerary practice, when the most valuable items were always placed on the body.

The very early origin of the custom of providing grave-goods prompted the rapid development of tomb-robbing, which even in Predynastic times was widespread and a serious threat to the long-term survival of burials in an undisturbed state. Most graves were robbed to some extent for the sake of the more valuable objects; the pottery vases were often left behind after any jewellery had been removed. In the course of tomb-robbing the burials were inevitably disturbed and many excavated graves have been found in which the bones of the skeleton lay in disarray. More curious are certain Predynastic graves in which the bones had been deposited in tidy but separate groups in different parts of the burial-pit, a situation noted occasionally in graves which appeared to show no evidence of plundering. Petrie argued that this showed there was some kind of dismemberment of the body prior to burial, and even suggested that a form of ritual cannibalism may have occurred, but this theory has not been generally accepted. It is possible that the collected groups of bones were reburials of disturbed remains from robbed graves, where the damage had been detected and an attempt made to collect the scattered human remains.

Despite the steady expansion of Upper Egyptian culture during the Late Predynastic Period, the individual character of the northern Predynastic farming communities was not completely extinguished until the unification of the country at the close of the Naqada III phase. The latest stages of the northern culture are represented at the site of Maadi, south of modern Cairo and not far distant from the settlement at El-Omari, which was established earlier. The occupation of Maadi overlapped with the Naqada II and Naqada III periods, and traded Upper Egyptian products, such as pottery vessels and slate palettes, have been found in the settlement. But the character of the Maadi community was quite different from the Naqada culture, consisting of a settlement containing not only oval or circular houses but also some underground dwellings such as occur in Palestine. The local pottery was mostly plain, following the Lower Egyptian tradition, with few polished red or black vessels, although imports from Syria–Palestine suggest a flourishing trade. Copper seems to have been worked at the site, perhaps with ore brought from Sinai. On the edges of the village were storage areas with underground cellars or large pottery store-jars set into the ground, the main purpose of the latter being the storage of food. The cellars may have been intended for the storage of goods, one example having been found to contain stone vases and carnelian beads. Trade in a wide range of goods was the basis of the local economy and the settlement flourished until about 3100 BC when the kings of Upper Egypt brought the area under their control. In recent years Predynastic remains bearing similarities to those of Maadi have been found in the Delta, at Buto in the west and at a small site called Tell Farkha in the east, suggesting that the Lower Egyptian style of Predynastic settlement may well have been widespread in the region before the adoption of the customs from the south.

3

The Unification of the Land

The process of unification of Egypt at the end of the Predynastic Period took place in two stages: the spread of a uniform material culture throughout the country on the one hand, and the establishment of unified political control on the other. There is considerable evidence that the former was achieved well before political union, by the diffusion of products characteristic of the latest stage of the Naqada culture to all areas. Later Egyptian tradition contains references to the existence of primitive separate kingdoms of the north and south, based at Buto and Hierakonpolis respectively, but there is not yet sufficient archaeological evidence to show what form of political control was present in these power centres, or whether their rulers can truly be considered as kings.

The importance of Hierakonpolis has long been recognised, since the excavations of J.E. Quibell and F.W. Green at the site in 1897–9 produced a mass of evidence bearing on the period of unification, including the famous ceremonial palette of Narmer. This object, often taken to be a record of the definitive victory of the southern kingdom over the north, will be discussed below in a consideration of the political aspects of unification. More recent excavations at Hierakonpolis have confirmed that it was a major urbanised centre of the Naqada culture and a residence of powerful Upper Egyptian chiefs. This would fit very well with the Egyptian tradition of a southern kingdom, but the northern half of the picture is as yet incomplete, since exploration of the Delta site of Buto for early evidence has only recently commenced. Despite great difficulties, an expedition of the German Archaeological Institute under the direction of Dr Thomas von der Way has managed to overcome the problems of high subsoil water in order to reach the early strata at Buto. Predynastic remains have been successfully excavated there, illustrative of a culture of different character from the Naqada civilisation of Upper Egypt and suggesting that there was indeed a Lower Egyptian Predynastic centre at Buto. The Predynastic settlements at the sites of Merimde, El-Omari and Maadi, described in earlier chapters, also exhibit individual styles of pottery and other artefacts unlike those found in the south. The Predynastic finds so far discovered at Buto resemble those from the site of Maadi, with which they are approximately contemporary. This collected evidence shows that Lower Egypt did possess its own unique material culture which was eventually submerged by the spread of the Upper Egyptian tradition. Further work at Buto, and perhaps at other Delta sites, may help to improve our knowledge of the northern Predynastic sequence and establish whether the tradition of a Lower Egyptian Predynastic kingdom can be confirmed.

The steady percolation of the typical products of the Naqada culture into the northern part of Egypt during the Naqada II and Naqada III periods was an important part of the unification process. Typical pottery and objects of this age are known at some sites very far to the north, such as Minshat Abu Omar in the eastern Delta. At this site a cemetery has been discovered containing graves of classic Naqada III style, with funerary goods no different from those which might be expected in burials of the same period in Upper Egyptian sites. Recent exploration of the Nile Delta has produced evidence for the introduction of the Naqada III culture at a number of locations in the eastern part of the region, including Tell Samara, Tell er-Roba, Kufr Nigm, Tell Farkha and Tell Ibrahim Awad. At many of these sites material of the early dynasties also occurs, especially funerary objects in graves of characteristic First-Dynasty type. The names of Scorpion and Narmer occur on pottery vessels from Minshat Abu Omar, and recently the names of Ka and Narmer have been reported from Tell Ibrahim Awad. The most informative new evidence on the spread of typical Naqada products into the Delta was, however, found as recently as 1989 in the excavations at Buto. The careful excavation of deep stratified deposits from the period of the unification of the land has revealed a fascinating sequence of material, which does much to illustrate the replacement of the Lower Egyptian Predynastic culture by that of Upper Egypt. The earliest stratum so far reached contained typical ceramics of Lower Egypt, the pottery of the Maadi culture. Above this was a layer described by the excavators as 'transitional', which still contained vessels of traditional Lower Egyptian types but manufactured in the style of Naqada pottery. Fragments of true Naqada imports also appeared in this level, but they became very common in the higher levels of the stratified deposits. An analysis of the relative quantities of northern and southern pottery types showed a dramatic change within the Late Predynastic Period as the proportion of southern pottery jumped from around 2 per cent of the total to about 40 per cent and then continued to rise until it constituted 99 per cent in the strata of Naqada III date.

Although the archaeological sequence found at Buto has shown that Upper Egyptian culture arrived in the Delta by the late Naqada II stage in around 3300 BC, the bulk of Naqada products so far found in the Delta region belong to Naqada III, the terminal phase of the Predynastic Period. The characteristics of this age are well known from burial sites excavated in Upper Egypt a long time ago, but in the early days the graves from the final part of the Predynastic Period were not always distinguished from those of Naqada II. In some cases the latest burials were identified by the use of Petrie's sequence dates, or they were called 'Late Gerzean', 'Protodynastic' or 'Semainian', old terms explained in the

30 Cylindrical pottery vase inscribed with the name of the Late Predynastic king Ka, one of the Upper Egyptian rulers at the period of unification. About 3150 BC. From Abydos. H. 27 cm.

Introduction to this book. Under these heads were grouped numerous burials ranging from the end of the Naqada II period down to well within the First Dynasty. Thanks to the work of Werner Kaiser on the chronology of the Naqada culture, it is possible to reassess the contents of individual graves, assuming that they have been sufficiently well documented, and to place the material at its correct relative point. In this manner, many burials of the Naqada III phase can be identified among the published graves from old excavations.

Some of the most elaborate graves found at sites such as Naqada or El-Amra can be shown to belong to the very end of the Predynastic Period, when the architecture of the tombs and the style of the contents foreshadow the customs of the First Dynasty. As explained in the foregoing chapter, the pottery of the last stage of the Predynastic Period shows differences from that of Naqada II, chiefly because of a great expansion in the use of the drab, utilitarian fabric to which Petrie gave the name 'late ware'. This clay was used for bowls and small vases, but particularly for tall jars which are a characteristic feature of the grave-goods with Naqada III burials. The decorated pottery of Naqada II declined rapidly and all the complex painted scenes disappear, leaving only a few types of vessel with red-painted lines or irregular marks. It is at this period that the wavy-handled jars lose their functional handles and acquire instead a mere ridge of clay. The very latest stage of this development is seen in the cylindrical jars in which even the ridge has been lost, to be replaced by an incised or painted line. These cylinder jars appear at the very end of the Predynastic Period and continue into the First Dynasty, some examples being conveniently dated by the presence of ink inscriptions giving the names of the Late Predynastic king Ka, or of Aha in the First Dynasty itself.

The cylindrical pottery vessels resembled certain popular First-Dynasty stone vases and the similarity was deliberately enhanced, probably so that the pottery jars could be considered economical substitutes for the stone ones. This set off a new line of development in the stone vessels, in which the line around the neck of the vase was reinterpreted as a piece of cord, which in the finest examples is indicated by detailed cross-hatching. Over the long history of these jars the indication of the cord became less well executed, declining once again to a ridge before disappearing completely. Pottery and calcite examples of cylinder jars have often been found together in graves dating to the end of the Naqada III period and commencement of the First Dynasty. The familiar black-topped pottery of Naqada I–II had fallen out of use, but some red polished and rough ware vases still occurred down to the very end of the Predynastic Period.

Of the other grave-goods, the cosmetic palettes at the beginning of the First Dynasty had been simplified to rectangular or oval forms, occasionally with incised lines around the edges as a kind of decorative border. That they were still used for their original purpose of grinding cosmetic is shown by examples which bear the green stain of crushed malachite. The great ceremonial palettes with relief decoration, which are a feature of the period of unification, were never destined for funerary use but were votive objects kept in the temples. Stone vases became increasingly common in graves of the Naqada III period, as did objects of copper.

The latest Predynastic graves show clear affinities with small tombs of

31 Copper harpoon blade, with traces of the original attachment to the haft. Late Predynastic, about 3300 BC. From Mahasna. L. 15.5 cm.

32 One face of the ceremonial palette of King Narmer, carved with a relief showing the king with a defeated captive, probably representative of a northern enemy. Included in the decoration of the other side of the palette is a scene in which the king, preceded by the standards of different districts, inspects the decapitated bodies of enemies. Early First Dynasty, about 3100 BC. From Hierakonpolis. H. 63 cm. Cairo, Egyptian Museum.

the early First Dynasty in the selection of a rectangular shape for the burial-pit and the increasingly common use of mud-brick or wooden lining. In some late Predynastic tombs the pit is subdivided by a partition wall to create a separate area for some of the grave-goods, a practice first seen in the 'Painted Tomb' of Hierakonpolis. Following the unification of the country, the development of multiple rooms in the substructure was accelerated and a plan introduced which placed a pair of chambers at one or both ends of the grave. In this manner a suite of three or five rooms was created, in which the central one contained the burial. Examples of this pattern are common in cemeteries from the early part of the First Dynasty, such as Naga ed-Der, Tura and El-Amra. The same basic plan

sometimes occurs in conjunction with some very large mastaba super-structures, such as tomb 3503 at Saqqara. It should be remembered that the destruction of the superstructures of Late Predynastic graves gives the misleading impression that the tombs were small and insignificant. The finest brick-lined Late Predynastic graves have been found at Abydos, not far from the royal cemetery of the First Dynasty, as described in the next chapter.

Just as the material culture became increasingly uniform, political unification seems also to have been achieved by a steady process of evolution rather than by a sudden dramatic change. Much of the discussion of this topic has been influenced by the decorated palette of Narmer from Hierakonpolis, which has been conveniently regarded as the principal record of Narmer's final victory over the north. This may be a correct interpretation, but is not necessarily so, and the increasing evidence for a gradual process of unification over some 200 years makes the idea of a single set-piece battle less likely. Certainly there was conflict during the emergence of the unified state, as shown by evidence from other decorated palettes, but there were probably numerous battles and skirmishes as rival chiefs struggled for territory. Some of the conflict recorded on the palettes may in any case have been directed against tribes from desert regions outside the Nile Valley rather than being

33 Part of a ceremonial palette (the 'Towns' palette) with a relief showing animals, possibly representing different clan groups, destroying walled settlements. Late Predynastic to First Dynasty, about 3100 BC. H. 18.5 cm. Cairo, Egyptian Museum.

34 Part of a ceremonial palette (the 'Battlefield' palette) with relief decoration showing a scene of captives and slain victims of battle, being preyed upon by wild animals. The fragment at the top left is a cast of a piece in the Ashmolean Museum, Oxford. Late Predynastic to First Dynasty, about 3100 BC. H. 32.8 cm.

connected with internal disputes. That the different urban centres in the country were fortified is shown by the so-called Towns palette, on which a number of settlements are shown under siege. The attacking forces are represented by animal symbols, perhaps representative of individual districts, and they are shown hacking their way into the fortified enclosures of the enemy. These enclosures must have consisted of mud-brick defensive walls, providing the earliest evidence for the use of brick as a building material on a large scale.

The ceremonial palettes seem to have evolved from the earlier functional versions, which were intended for grinding cosmetics. It is possible that some of the Predynastic palettes in the shapes of animals, which occurred regularly in the Naqada I period, had already developed a magical significance and that their exotic forms were not simply for

decorative purposes. A relic of the original function of the objects remains even on the grandest of the decorated versions, including the Narmer palette, in the presence of an enclosed circular depression for the grinding of cosmetics, although no longer used for so prosaic a purpose. On the Narmer palette this area has been linked into the relief decoration by enclosing it between the intertwined necks of two mythical beasts, whilst the Hunters palette in the British Museum has a more simple raised ring. The large palettes were, it seems, made to be placed in temples as votive objects.

Much importance has been attached to the fact that Narmer is shown wearing the White Crown on one side of his palette and the Red Crown on the other, suggesting that he was claiming to rule the two parts of Egypt represented by those crowns. Although this may be a correct

35 The other side of the palette shown in Fig. 34, decorated with a relief of two long-necked gazelles browsing on a date-palm.

36 Relief scene on the mace-head of King Scorpion from Hierakonpolis. Late Predynastic, about 3100 BC.

interpretation, some caution is required since we are not certain at what date the Red Crown became associated with Lower Egypt; the first known depiction of this emblem in fact comes from Naqada in the south. The motif on one side of the palette which links a defeated captive, trampled down by a falcon, and a sign showing reeds is generally taken to be a graphic statement that the king, represented by the falcon, had defeated the marsh-dwellers of Lower Egypt. It is less clear just who these people were, as they do not look particularly Egyptian. On several of the other decorated palettes of the period they appear again in the roles of enemies or prisoners; they are depicted with curled hair and beards, and are circumcised, but they do not look the same as the Egyptians who are shown, for example, on the Hunters palette. It is possible that some of the warfare conducted against the north around the time of Narmer may have been directed against a local population which had moved into the Delta from the west, and who were regarded by the Upper Egyptian rulers as outsiders.

In some cases defeated enemies are identified by icons which are familiar in the repertoire of later Egyptian art, but it cannot be assumed that their significance in the Late Predynastic Period remained the same as in much later reliefs. An example is the large ceremonial mace-head from Hierakonpolis of King Scorpion, possibly the predecessor of Narmer, which bears reliefs showing the king participating in some kind of official ceremony. In the upper register are several standards of different districts with dead birds of the kind known as *rekhyt* hanging from them. This seems to imply that the king, with his allies represented by the standards, defeated the *Rekhyt*-people, always identified in later times with the Egyptian population. But we do not know what was signified by the term *rekhyt* at the beginning of Egyptian history, and some authorities believe that they were originally Libyans. They may, however, have constituted the population of the Delta, a region which always had a tendency to attract settlers from the west. Consequently, documents like the Scorpion mace-head or the Narmer palette, which have been regarded as commemorating the internal conflict through which the unification of the land was achieved, from the point of view of the Upper Egyptian kings may have been records of the defeat of foreigners. Probably much of the process of conquest was completed by the little-known rulers of Upper Egypt at the end of the Predynastic Period, who, in addition to Scorpion, included individuals named Ka and Iryhor. This would have left Narmer to consolidate the success and perhaps turn his attention to different tribes in the more remote quarters of the land.

Major fragments of two well-known palettes of the unification period are in the British Museum, one decorated with scenes of hunting and the other with images of captives and slain victims of battle. In view of this decoration, these objects are commonly known as the Hunters and the Battlefield palettes. On the former, companies of warriors dressed in kilts are seen hunting wild animals, particularly lions, which are shown pierced by arrows. The Battlefield palette also bears a relief of a lion, but

37 Fragmentary ceremonial palette (the 'Hunters' palette) decorated with scenes of groups of warriors hunting lions and other wild animals. The fragment on the left is a cast of a piece in the Louvre. Late Predynastic to First Dynasty, about 3100 BC. L. 66.8 cm.

in this case depicted as a scavenger preying upon the bodies of the slain after a battle, in the company of the vultures. The human figures on this relief resemble the defeated enemies on the great palette of Narmer. Towards the centre of the Battlefield palette were figures of prisoners, one restrained by a figure in a long cloak and two others held by the standards of the falcon and ibis. (This part of the decoration is on a fragment of the palette in the Ashmolean Museum, Oxford.) Unlike the Hunters palette, the Battlefield palette is decorated on both faces, the reverse with figures of two long-necked gazelles browsing on a palm tree.

Some elements in the decoration of the slate palettes show affinities with the art style of early Mesopotamia, in such motifs as the intertwined necks of mythical beasts. The decorated handle of an ivory knife from Gebel el-Arak bears a figure subduing two lions, a motif in which some have seen links with the epic of Gilgamesh. A similar representation occurs at an earlier date in the decoration of the 'Painted Tomb' at Hierakonpolis, considered to be the burial place of a local Predynastic ruler. During the period of unification, several other features which appear quite suddenly in the Nile Valley also have Mesopotamian links, examples being the development of a particular style of recessed brick architecture, the use of cylinder seals and the emergence of writing itself. Examples of imported Mesopotamian cylinder seals have been found in graves of the Naqada II period, and copies were made in Egypt. It is possible that some form of contact between Egypt and early Mesopotamia occurred through the desert route now known as the Wadi Hammamat, which leads from the Nile in Upper Egypt to the Red Sea. Interestingly,

38 Elevation and plan of the elaborate panelled system of brickwork, known as 'palace-façade', used in First-Dynasty architecture.

this route meets the Nile opposite the site of Naqada, the centre of the Upper Egyptian Predynastic civilisation and the location of a major town by the end of the Predynastic Period.

The architectural term for the embellishment of brick walls with a regular pattern of recesses and buttresses is 'palace-façade'. The style originated from an attempt to reproduce in brick the appearance of more primitive structures made from reed matting (such buildings were still used until relatively recent times by the Marsh Arabs of Iraq). In the reed buildings, the panelling of the exterior was necessitated by the nature of the material: projecting bundles of reeds had to be added to screen-walls in order to give the required strength and rigidity. The façades of brick buildings copied the effect in a formalised manner, with regularly placed 38 deep recesses separated by simpler niches. The design became intimately linked with royalty through the use of one element – an individual compound niche – as the surrounding frame in which royal names were written, known as the *serekh*, an Egyptian term with the meaning 'to make known'. This is normally shown with the falcon of the god Horus perched above, and became the so-called Horus-name of the king, one of the several parts of the royal titulary of later periods (see above, p.15). Most of the royal inscriptions of the Early Dynastic Period give the Horus-

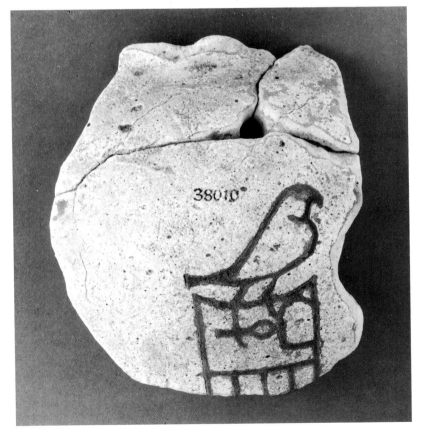

39 Example of the writing of the royal name Aha in the frame of the *serekh*, as was usual in the Early Dynastic Period. First Dynasty, about 3000 BC. H. 14 cm.

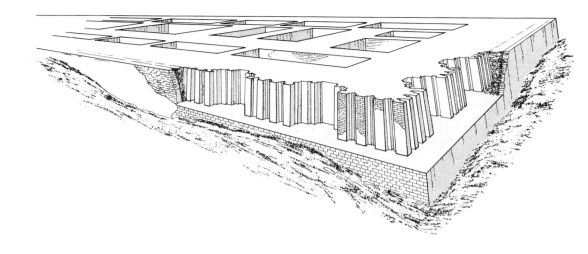

40 Part of the superstructure of the tomb of Queen Neithhotep at Naqada, one of the earliest of the palace-façade mastaba tombs. First Dynasty, about 3100 BC.

name of the king, but from the reign of Den the first use of the *nsw-bit* name appears, the element of the royal titulary most frequently used in later texts.

The *serekh* appears in rough inscriptions on pottery jars at the end of the Predynastic Period, with the names of the kings Ka and Scorpion, who ruled immediately prior to the beginning of the First Dynasty. In some of these early examples, the Horus-falcon is not shown. The more formal inscriptions on the tombstones of the First-Dynasty kings are sufficiently detailed to show the panelled design within the *serekh*. 39 Placing the king's name within the panelled frame is considered to be a graphic device showing the royal presence in the palace, which the niched façade is supposed to represent. This hypothesis is based in part on the Third-Dynasty Step Pyramid complex of Djoser, which has a panelled wall thought to be modelled on that of the royal palace in Memphis. The only Early Dynastic evidence for the use of this form of architecture in palaces, however, comes from the excavation of a doorway in a panelled wall of the First Dynasty in the town of Hierakonpolis, possibly a small surviving part of a royal palace.

The palace-façade is far better represented in funerary architecture, since it was adopted for the superstructures of large mastaba tombs of the First Dynasty. The reason for its use in these non-royal monuments may have been that the façades of the tombs were copying the panelling which was a feature of the royal funerary enclosures at Abydos. Immediately following the period of unification, some large tombs with niched façades were constructed at the old Predynastic centre of Naqada, one of which survived in reasonable condition to be excavated in 1896. 40 The location of this monument at Naqada is an interesting link between the end of the Predynastic Period and the beginning of the First Dynasty.

It was built in the reign of Aha for the burial of Queen Neithhotep, whose name appears on small ivory labels found in the tomb. The purpose of these labels was quite mundane: they were attached to items of jewellery in the burial equipment, and bear numerals recording the number of beads on a necklace. Neithhotep may have been the mother of King Aha, whose name occurred on two wooden labels from the tomb.

Following the foundation of the capital at Memphis at the beginning of the First Dynasty, the focus of attention moved away from Naqada to the royal cemetery at Abydos and the large tombs of officials at Saqqara. Many of the latter had palace-façade superstructures, although this style of building which appeared at the period of unification gradually decreased in popularity. In this it matches the pattern shown by some of the other innovations which appeared at the time of unification, such as the use of cylinder seals, showing a decline in use but without disappearing entirely.

Writing is now known to have appeared in Egypt before the time of Narmer. New evidence from Abydos has shown that written records of funerary equipment, similar to the labels of Neithhotep mentioned above, already existed during the terminal phase of the Naqada culture. The inscriptions on the earliest available documents are extremely concise, with some evidence for the use of abbreviations. This is not what we might expect from a system of writing in the process of development; rather, it suggests that the script was already subject to certain rules which had been established at an even earlier stage. If, as is suspected,

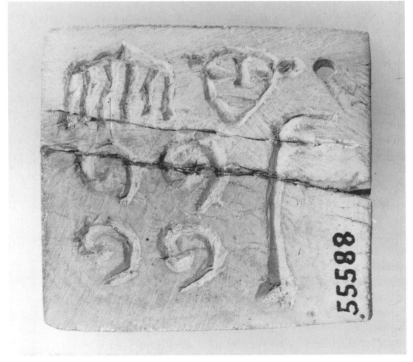

41 Small ivory label from the tomb of Queen Neithhotep at Naqada, with an inscription recording the number of beads on a necklace in the tomb equipment. First Dynasty, about 3000 BC. H. 2.2 cm.

the idea of writing was borrowed from early Mesopotamia, it is not too surprising that the development stage seems to be missing in Egypt. The early written records of the Nile Valley are not to be considered simply as primitive ideograms, since it is evident that elements of the phonetic system, with aspects of the grammar and syntax known from later periods, were already in place. A misleading impression has been given by the nature of the documents which have survived, which were relatively trivial items at the time, and many of which now exist in a fragmentary condition.

The small ivory labels used to identify tomb equipment from the end of the Predynastic Period gave rise after the unification to larger versions which served the same function but which also bore inscriptions recording historical events. At the same time there was a great expansion in the use of seals, reflecting two developments: the increasingly formal structure of the administration of the land and the greatly increased quantities of produce going into the burial equipment of rich tombs. These matters are considered in more detail in the next chapter.

4

The Early Dynasties

As was explained in the foregoing chapter, the transition from the Late Predynastic Period into the First Dynasty now appears to have been a far less dramatic event than was previously supposed. Rather than a sudden conquest as the outcome of one or two battles, a picture emerges of the steady percolation of the authority of the Upper Egyptian Predynastic rulers to extend over the whole country. From such a position, the establishment of the line of kings which we identify, after the later king-lists, with the First Dynasty, may have been no more than a formal confirmation of the existing situation.

Egyptian tradition states that the first king of Egypt was Menes, who founded Memphis as his capital, and there has been much discussion over the identity of this king. It is quite possible that the name Menes was derived from the Egyptian word *mn*, 'to endure, to be permanent', used in later times as a designation for the founder of the state, whose true identity had been forgotten. There is, however, an ivory label from the palace-façade tomb at Naqada with an inscription apparently giving the word *mn* as the *nbty*-name of a king, in conjunction with the *serekh* of Aha. Some have taken this to mean that Aha and Menes were the same

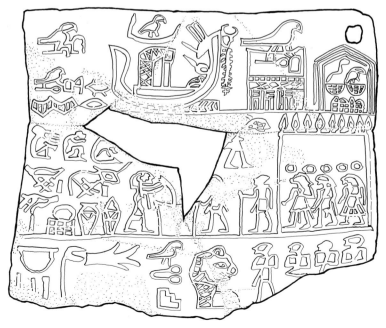

42 Inscription on an ivory label for an oil-jar, with a record of events in the reign of King Aha. The top register contains the hieroglyph *mn* at the right-hand side; this has been linked with Menes, named in later Egyptian sources as the founder of the First Dynasty. From the tomb of Queen Neithhotep at Naqada. About 3100 BC.

63

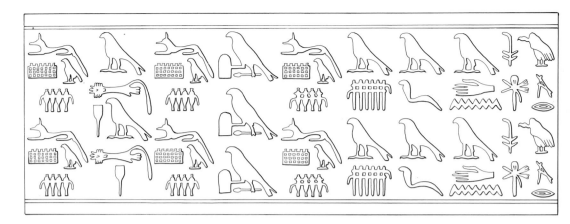

43 Reconstruction of the text of a clay seal-impression from the royal cemetery at Abydos, giving the names of First-Dynasty rulers from Narmer to Den in their historical order. About 3000 BC.

person, whilst an alternative view exists, that the label commemorates the funeral of Aha's predecessor, perhaps Narmer, who should be identified as Menes. In view of the increasing evidence for the cultural unity of the land at an earlier stage than used to be supposed, the resolution of this argument is of minor importance. We already have a sequence of kings for the First Dynasty, established through the work of Flinders Petrie on the re-excavation of the royal tombs at Abydos in 1899–1900, and recently confirmed by a splendid discovery which resulted from a meticulous examination of the same site by the German Archaeological Institute at Cairo. A clay seal-impression has been recovered with inscriptions giving the names of the kings of the First Dynasty in chronological order from Narmer down to Den, with the addition of the name of Queen Merneith and that of Khentamentiu, the principal god of Abydos.

The monuments from the reign of Narmer have already been described in Chapter 3, in the discussion of the unification of Egypt. This king was probably buried in tomb B17/18 at Abydos, a double-chamber tomb typical of the early phase of the royal cemetery. The successors of Narmer were named Aha, Djer, Djet, Den, Anedjib, Semerkhet and Qa-a. In addition, there exists at Abydos a tomb for an individual named Merneith, whose position has only recently been confirmed. Since names compounded with the name of the goddess Neith were generally those of females in the Early Dynastic Period, it was assumed that Merneith must have been a queen who ruled independently for a period and therefore qualified for burial in the royal necropolis. This theory has gained substantial support from the discovery of the remarkable seal-impressions, mentioned above, in which she is given the title 'King's Mother' and appears in the sequence of First-Dynasty rulers. She was probably the mother of Den and may have acted as regent before his accession.

Of the political history of the Early Dynastic Period we know very little, owing to the lack of substantial historical texts. Some references to events in the reigns of the kings of the first two dynasties are recorded in the inscriptions on the Palermo Stone and, with a greater degree of confusion, in the *History* of Manetho. The beginning of the First Dynasty, under King Aha, seems to have been a time during which the recent unification of the country was consolidated and some attempts were made to extend the authority of the king to the south, if the interpretation of an ebony label from Abydos as a record of a Nubian campaign is correct. Another label commemorates the foundation of a religious sanctuary of the goddess Neith, probably at her later centre of Sais in the Delta. The same southern and northern areas of the kingdom also received attention in the reign of Djer, successor of Aha: a rock-inscription of the king near Wadi Halfa indicates considerable expansion of Egyptian authority to the south, whilst an ivory label from Abydos records a royal visit to Buto and Sais. An expedition to the east, probably to Sinai, is documented on the Palermo Stone.

Apart from funerary monuments, the name of Djet occurs only in an inscription in the desert to the east of Edfu, probably cut during some trading or mining expedition. A magnificent limestone stela with the royal *serekh* was found at the king's tomb at Abydos and the two rich mastaba tombs Saqqara 3504 and Giza V are known to date from his reign: they probably belonged to high officials.

The reign of Den was marked by a number of new practices and technical developments, the latter being exploited for the enhancement of the king's tomb. In addition to the usual *serekh*-panel containing the Horus-name of the king, the *nsw-bit* name first appears (see above, Chapter 3), probably to be read Semti. The king is depicted on a wooden

44 The text from a wooden label for a jar of oil from the tomb equipment of King Aha, with supplementary inscriptions recording a visit to a sanctuary of the goddess Neith. First Dynasty, about 3000 BC. From Abydos.

65

label from Abydos, now in the British Museum, wearing the Double Crown of Upper and Lower Egypt in the performance of a ritual associated with his jubilee. The appearance of the Double Crown in this scene is appropriate, since the jubilee or Sed-festival reconfirmed the king's possession of the land as far as its furthest limits. On the same label the name of an official called Hemaka occurs, with the title 'Seal-bearer of the King of Lower Egypt', a position which was to remain one of the great offices of state in later Egyptian history. The name of Hemaka occurs widely on labels and seal-impressions from the reign, many of them from tomb 3035 at Saqqara in which Hemaka was probably buried. Another official, named Ankhka, also served under Den. Although the name of Den is lost from the Palermo Stone, some events from his reign do seem to be recorded, including the jubilee festival of the Abydos label. References also occur to several other religious festivals and to a military campaign against tribesmen, perhaps the event depicted on an ivory label in the British Museum, with a carving of the king and an Asiatic prisoner.

Political conditions under the next two rulers, Anedjib and Semerkhet, are far from clear. Inscriptions of the former on stone vases from Abydos had been erased by Semerkhet, suggesting some kind of disfavour of the kind frequently encountered in the later history of Dynastic Egypt. Anejdib had the *nsw-bit* title Merpabia; he was buried in tomb x at Abydos, a small structure notable for its well-preserved wooden floor.

45 Ebony label with a scene showing part of the jubilee festival of King Den, in which the king ran between markers representing the boundaries of Egypt. The primary use of the label was as an identification tag for a jar of oil. First Dynasty, about 2900 BC. From Abydos. H. 5.5 cm.

46 Ivory label for a jar of oil, with inscriptions recording religious events of the reign of King Semerkhet. First Dynasty, about 2900 BC. From Abydos. H. 3.4 cm.

Semerkhet added to his *nsw-bit* title another element, the 'Two Ladies' or *nbty*-name, another standard part of the later royal titulary. With both these titles the king adopted the name Irynetjer, as written on a small ivory label in the British Museum. This label is of interest in depicting a baboon divinity with the name Hedjwer, 'Great White', in honour of whom votive figures were placed in the archaic temples of Abydos, Hierakonpolis and Elephantine. The name of the official Henuka on this label has also been found on documents from the succeeding reign, showing that Henuka lived on to serve under Qa-a, the last king of the First Dynasty.

The sequence of kings at the beginning of the Second Dynasty is preserved in an inscription on the shoulder of a granite statue in the Egyptian Museum, Cairo, which lists the names Hetepsekhemwy, Raneb and Ninetjer in what is probably the correct order. No tombs of these kings exist in the royal necropolis at Abydos, but sealings with their names have been recovered from the underground galleries of two extensive tombs at Saqqara. Two very obscure kings, named Weneg and Sened respectively, followed Ninetjer; stone vases inscribed with their names are known, but most of the evidence for their existence comes from the king-lists and from other post-Second-Dynasty material, particularly a Fourth-Dynasty tomb at Saqqara whose owner bore the title of 'Overseer of Priests of Sened'. This individual also served in the cult of the next king, Peribsen, who is generally thought to have been the same ruler who bore the Horus-name Sekhemib. The name Peribsen was preceded by the animal of the god Seth, but the reasons for the adoption

of this alternative title remain obscure, although it is possible that there was some kind of political or religious dispute.

The next king to have left monuments was named Khasekhem, who is portrayed in some fine statues from Hierakonpolis, but this name also occurs with a dual ending in the form Khasekhemwy. It is generally accepted that both forms of the name refer to the same ruler, and it has been surmised that the king might have adopted the new form after he had resolved the dispute between the Horus and Seth followers. Support for this theory is found in the existence of some clay seal-impressions of the reign, which include the phrase, 'the Two Lords are at peace with him', taken to imply that the gods Horus and Seth were now united; indeed the animal representatives of both gods are shown together above the frame of the royal *serekh* on these seals. The monuments from the reign of Khasekhem/Khasekhemwy anticipate the more regular and formal style expected from Egyptian art of the Old Kingdom. The hieroglyphs on the clay seal-impressions are arranged in a more ordered fashion than those on earlier seals, and the statues from Hierakonpolis are shown seated in a pose soon to become conventional. They are depicted in the robe of the jubilee festival and wearing the crown of Upper Egypt; on the bases of the sculptures are inscriptions recording numbers of enemies killed. Similar themes of victory are inscribed on the remains of a stela of the king and three large stone vessels, also found at Hierakonpolis. All these monuments bear the early form of the king's name, but a granite door-jamb has beeen recovered from Hierakonpolis with the form Khasekhemwy. This inscription again shows a fine regular arrangement of the hieroglyphs, such as occurs on monuments from the Third and Fourth Dynasties.

The archaeological record of the early dynasties is dominated by funerary material, due in part to the pattern of early excavation, which was concentrated on cemetery sites. Only in recent years has Early Dynastic material begun to be revealed in settlement contexts, where it is often difficult to reach owing to the presence of overlying later structures or silt deposits. This is certainly true of ancient Memphis, where the tombs of Saqqara and Helwan have survived in a reasonable state of preservation, but the remains of the First-Dynasty town seem to lie deeply buried under the valley alluvium. Survey work carried out by an expedition of the Egypt Exploration Society suggests that the early town may have been situated to the north-west of the visible ruins of later Memphis, closer to the desert escarpment where the great palace-façade tombs of high officials were built. One interesting result of recent excavation has been the discovery of Early Dynastic remains in the Delta, where the recovery of such material was once thought to be impossible. Much of this Delta evidence has once again proved to be of a funerary nature, for the simple reason that the cemeteries were placed on high-lying land which has remained above the level of more recent silt deposits. To dig through the alluvium down to the depth required to reach Early Dynastic settlements is a difficult matter, and major pumping equipment may be required to take off the subsoil water, as in

47 Limestone statue of King Khasekhemwy, one of a pair from the site of Hierakonpolis in Upper Egypt. Second Dynasty, about 2700 BC. H. 62 cm. Oxford, Ashmolean Museum.

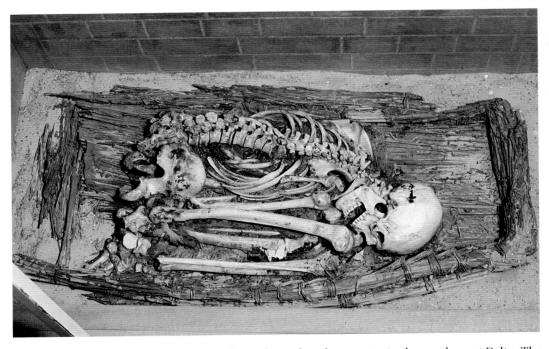

48 Contracted burial in a basketwork coffin, from a grave cut into the superstructure of a large brick tomb of the First Dynasty at Tarkhan. About 2900 BC.

excavations at Buto, the early urban centre in the north-west Delta. The effort may, however, be rewarded with important discoveries: at Buto the German excavators have found remains of mud-brick buildings of the Second and Third Dynasties. Discoveries of equally early material have been made at the other end of the Nile Valley, at Elephantine, where a walled town developed from the Early Dynastic Period into the Old Kingdom. Seal-impressions with the names of kings from the Second and Third Dynasties have been found in the remains of this settlement.

The Early Dynastic cemeteries of the Delta are very similar in tomb design and contents to those of Upper Egypt, although no really large tombs have yet been found in the far north. Typical grave-goods of the period are stone and pottery vessels – the latter almost exclusively plain and utilitarian in contrast to the decorated pottery of the Predynastic Period – bone arrowheads, copper tools, ivory and stone amulets and gaming-pieces. Flint implements still appear, side by side with the copper tools, but the quality of the flintwork is not so fine as it had been in the Late Predynastic Period. The decline in technique can be traced through the early dynasties and on into the Old Kingdom, although flint as a material for tools was never totally replaced in ancient Egypt.

The desert fringes of the Nile Valley are rich in Early Dynastic cemetery sites, many of which were excavated on a large scale in the early years of the twentieth century. These sites have provided the basis of our knowledge of the burial customs of the period and the objects from the graves have illustrated almost every type of product. The styles of the tombs varied more according to the wealth of their owners than according to geographical area, as the masses attempted to imitate the tombs of the rich in so far as their resources allowed. The pace of development was therefore set by the rich, who quickly adopted the advantages of new tomb designs and included the latest products in their funerary equipment. Poor burials retained old customs much longer, such as the contracted position of the body, illustrated by a skeleton in a basketwork coffin from a grave at Tarkhan of the middle First Dynasty. Most cemeteries contained a mixture of burials from all levels of society, with the wealthier tombs covered by large brick superstructures whilst the poorer ones possessed simpler tumuli of brick or rubble, not too different from Late Predynastic graves. At sites such as Tarkhan, Helwan and Naga ed-Der the whole range of tomb types can be found, including the first appearance of features such as the offering-chapel, which were to determine the development of the tomb in the Old Kingdom. The most important cemeteries of all were those of Saqqara and Abydos, where the tombs of state officials and royalty were constructed.

Abydos and the Early Dynastic royal tombs

The archaeological site at Abydos in Upper Egypt is located in the low desert to the west of the Nile Valley, where it is backed by impressive limestone cliffs. Exploration of this site has shed light on all periods of Egyptian civilisation, but it is the Early Dynastic monuments which lie at the heart of its importance. Indeed, had it not been for the presence of the First-Dynasty tombs, many of the later antiquities for which Abydos is famous, such as the temples of Seti I and Ramesses II or the vast numbers of tomb-stelae of the Middle Kingdom, would never have been created. They were the products of a mistaken belief in later periods that the site had been the burial place of the god Osiris, a concept inspired by the presence of the archaic tombs, one of which – that of Djer – was converted into a model of the tomb of the god. The establishment of monuments at the site was considered to be advantageous in gaining favour from Osiris, most importantly a better chance of safe passage to the afterlife, and was the driving force behind the construction of royal and private cenotaphs and tombs. Offerings were taken in pottery jars to be left in the desert at the supposed tomb of the god, creating great deposits of pottery over the site of the First-Dynasty tombs in general and that of Djer in particular. The debris of these mounds gave rise to a modern Arabic name for the early royal necropolis, Umm el-Qaab, 'Mother of Pots'.

The early remains at Abydos include not only the tombs of kings from the First and Second Dynasties, but also the associated funerary enclosures situated some distance away, in which rituals connected with the cult of the dead kings were probably carried out. These structures are probably to be considered as the forerunners of the enclosure around the Third-Dynasty Step Pyramid of Djoser at Saqqara, with which they shared the common feature of palace-façade panelling. The site of the First Dynasty enclosures was investigated by Flinders Petrie in 1922, but the structures had been so destroyed that only the surrounding

49 Mud-brick ritual funerary enclosure of King Khasekhemwy at Abydos. Second Dynasty, about 2700 BC.

subsidiary graves were found, arranged in rows outside the enclosures and consequently betraying the position of the vanished buildings. These were burials of servants of the kings, killed to accompany their master, many more of whom were interred around the royal tombs themselves. A small part of the palace-façade wall of the enclosure of Merneith was discovered in a later excavation at the site, confirming that the buildings did indeed possess panelled façades. Despite the poor state of preservation of the First-Dynasty funerary enclosures, their form and architecture is illustrated on a larger scale by their Second-Dynasty counterparts, which still stand to a considerable height. Two of these have been investigated, and from seal-impressions found in the excavations they have been identifed as the ritual enclosures of Peribsen and Khasekhemwy. The monument of the latter king is the better preserved and its walls stand to a considerable height. A double wall ran around the perimeter of the enclosure, the inner one embellished with palace-façade panelling on the exterior. Just inside the entrances to both enclosures were small buildings which also had simplified niches along certain of their walls. It is of interest to note that the principal entrances to the enclosures lay at the south-east corner, the same point chosen for the entrances to the later Step Pyramid complexes.

Not far from the funerary enclosures is the site of the original temple of Abydos, in the ruins of which remains have been found of many periods of building, the result of a continual process of enlargement and renewal. The history of the temple goes back to the Early Dynastic Period, from which a number of discarded items of temple equipment have been recovered. They were found to have been dumped in a hole at a later period, presumably during some refurbishment of the temple which involved the clearing out of old material. Amongst the early objects were several glazed composition figures of baboons, probably intended as representations of the god called Hedjwer, 'Great White', whose appearance on a label of Semerkhet and on the Third-Dynasty reliefs of Djoser's pyramid has been mentioned above. Also in glazed composition, there were tiles for inlaying, model vessels, beads and part of a vase inscribed with the name of King Aha. The finest object from the group was an ivory figurine of a king wearing the White Crown and the cloak of the jubilee festival. It is not possible to establish precisely when the material in this dump was discarded and consequently the objects in it may cover a span of some considerable time. A similar cache in a temple at Elephantine has been shown to have been deposited in the Fifth Dynasty (about 2400 BC), when a collection of redundant items dating back to the First Dynasty was disposed of.

The royal cemetery of Abydos seems to have developed as an extension of a traditional burial ground of the Predynastic Period, in particular a

50 Palace-façade panelling from the funerary enclosure of King Khasekhemwy at Abydos (Fig. 49).

52 OPPOSITE Ivory
figure of a king in the
regalia of the jubilee
festival. Probably First
Dynasty, about 3100–
2890 BC. From Abydos.
H. 8.8 cm.

region known as Cemetery U, situated a little to the north of the tombs in Umm el-Qaab. This cemetery contains many graves of typical Predynastic pattern, dating from the Naqada I and II periods, but also later brick-lined tombs from the latest stage of the Predynastic Period, some of them being elaborate burial places with multiple rooms. Excavations by the German Archaeological Institute have shown that the sequence of tombs continues from the main area of Cemetery U in a southerly direction, towards the site of the royal tombs, and it has been suggested that certain of these tombs were constructed for the powerful Upper Egyptian rulers who were the immediate forerunners of the First Dynasty. Remains of rich burial equipment were found in these tombs, including many stone vessel fragments and both imported and local pottery, some with simple inscriptions. Amongst the latter were examples of the *serekh*-panel, well known in later times as the device in which royal names were inscribed. Most of the graves consisted of single brick-lined chambers, but one more elaborate tomb was found with no less than twelve rooms occupying a total area of 9.10 by 7.30 metres. Dated to the final stage of the Predynastic Period, this tomb had been built in two stages: the burial chamber at the north-west and the nine small storerooms on its eastern side were constructed first, and the two long rooms on the south added subsequently. Like all the early tombs of Abydos, the whole structure had been roofed with wood and reed matting.

51 An elaborate Late
Predynastic tomb at
Abydos, probably the
burial place of an
Upper Egyptian ruler.
About 3200 BC.

The contents of this tomb were remarkable, despite the fact that much

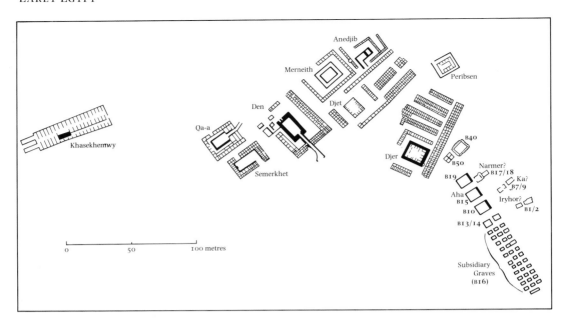

53 Plan of the royal cemetery of the First and Second Dynasties at Abydos.

had been lost by early plundering. Hundreds of pottery vessels had been placed in the storerooms, sorted according to type and including local products and imported vases from Canaan. Vases of the type with wavy ledge-handles at the sides were common, many of them with roughly painted inscriptions, among which were ideograms showing a scorpion and a tree. In the burial chamber there were traces of a wooden shrine and an ivory sceptre of the kind which formed part of the standard royal regalia of later times. Not far to the south of this tomb lie the earliest graves of the Abydos royal cemetery, so it would seem that the region south of the Predynastic Cemetery U came to be reserved for royal burials.

The first tombs of the royal cemetery lie in an area known as Cemetery B, a cluster of brick-lined pit-graves extending to the east of the larger tombs of the kings from the reign of Djer onwards. The most elaborate tomb of the group is that of Aha, partly because it was constructed in separate stages as improved versions of the final burial chamber were created, and partly owing to the presence for the first time of subsidiary graves for servants of the king. The first design seems to have been for a small tomb with two chambers, one placed immediately north of the other. This is a pattern which can be traced back in time to the predecessors of Aha, whose double-chamber tombs lie in the vicinity. In such tombs the southern chamber was intended for the burial and the northern one for the storage of additional funerary equipment. Three double-chamber tombs lie to the north of the complex of Aha, numbered B1/2, B9/7 and B17/18, and it has been suggested that these should be attributed to the kings Iryhor, Ka and Narmer. These attributions are plausible and have recently received support from the results of the re-excavation of the tombs by the German Archaeological Institute, in which seal-impressions and fragments from inscribed pottery vases with the name of Iryhor were recovered from tomb B1/2. The name of Narmer is of course well known from the great slate palette of the king found at Hierakonpolis, and although the rulers Ka and Iryhor are less familiar, there is, nevertheless, no doubt about the existence of the former, whilst for Iryhor there is limited evidence from early inscriptions. In the light of the recent excavations at Abydos, the distribution of the burials of the late Predynastic rulers and the first kings of Dynastic Egypt has been shown to fall into a highly logical pattern.

54 Subsidiary graves for the servants of King Aha, to the east of his tomb at Abydos. First Dynasty, about 3100 BC.

To return to the tomb of Aha, this was constructed on a far grander scale than any of the earlier burial places and is perhaps indicative of the increasing wealth available at the beginning of the First Dynasty. The original plan was for a traditional double-chamber tomb consisting of the chambers B13 and B14, but to the east of these a whole series of small subsidiary graves was added for the burial of slain servants. Skeletal remains from the area of these graves were uniformly of young individuals up to 25 years of age, confirming the theory that the servants of the king did not die a natural death. The presence of servant burials marked the start of a tradition which was to continue throughout the First Dynasty. At the west of the original royal tomb a new chamber was constructed (B10), followed by two more (B15 and B19), of which B15 was the one eventually used for the burial.

The tombs of the successors of Aha in the First Dynasty, together with two tombs from the Second Dynasty, lie a short distance to the west of Cemetery B. The burial chambers of these monuments became increasingly elaborate: although they still consisted essentially of a large brick-lined pit in the surface of the desert, the interior was frequently lined with wooden panelling and additional chambers for the storage of goods were incorporated. Around the main tomb were rows of small graves, now built in trenches in the form of linked cells of brickwork, to provide burial places for the servants. The numbers of subsidiary burials reached a peak in the middle of the dynasty, around the tombs of Djer and Djet. Grave-goods provided for these servant burials included not only pottery vessels but also copper tools, stone vessels and ivory carvings, and close to the vanished superstructures were rough inscribed limestone stelae giving the names of the occupants. From one of the

57 ABOVE Fragment of ivory from a box, inscribed with the name of King Aha and another personal name which may be read either Ima-ib or Bener-ib, probably the name of a queen. First Dynasty, about 3100 BC. From the tomb complex of Aha at Abydos. H. 3.1 cm.

55 OPPOSITE, ABOVE The brick-built tomb of King Den at Abydos, as partially re-excavated to reveal the subsidiary graves around the sand-filled main chamber. First Dynasty, about 3000 BC.

56 OPPOSITE, BELOW The funerary complex of King Aha at Abydos, consisting of brick-lined chambers sunk into the desert surface. First Dynasty, about 3100 BC.

subsidiary graves around the tomb of Qa-a came a set of limestone model vases, painted to imitate the appearance of hard stones, one of the earliest examples of the use of model substitutes in funerary equipment.

As has been mentioned already, the tomb of Djer was in later times converted into a cenotaph of the god Osiris, to which offerings were brought. When the tomb was excavated by Amélineau it was found to contain a stone image of the god, shown lying on a funerary couch, apparently placed there in the late Middle Kingdom when the Osiris cenotaph was refurbished. Despite this reuse of the tomb, remains of the original burial equipment had survived, the most remarkable discovery being the finding by Petrie of the remains of a human arm, wrapped in linen, on which was some original First-Dynasty jewellery. One of the bracelets consisted of a series of gold and lapis beads in the form of the royal *serekh*.

The earlier tombs of the cemetery, those of Djer, Djet and Queen Merneith, all lacked any entrance to the burial chamber except from above; consequently the roof and superstructure of the tombs could only be completed after the burial had been installed. In the reign of Den a significant advance was made with the invention of the descending stairway entrance, roofed over with wood. The same material was used for the main roofing of all the tombs, and traces of the original timber have been found collapsed into the grave-pits. Above the wooden roofs were the grave superstructures in the form of low square or rectangular tumuli or mastabas, cased with mud brick and surrounded by an enclosure wall. In front of the tomb was a pair of stone stelae inscribed with the name of the owner to mark the offering place. From an early date the stelae could be made of hard stones as an alternative to limestone, as in the case of the examples from the tombs of Djer, Semerkhet and Qa-a. The Second-Dynasty stelae of Peribsen, one of which is in the British Museum, were hammered out from compact slabs of gneiss.

Recent work at the tomb of Djet has shown that the mastaba superstructures incorporated two elements: a low brick-cased tumulus immediately over the burial chamber, but not rising above the surrounding ground level, with a second roof above covering the whole area of the tomb, over which was the larger mastaba. This inclusion of a hidden tumulus in the superstructure of the tomb is paralleled in the great First-Dynasty mastabas of Saqqara, but was not known to have existed at Abydos until 1988. Its presence reveals the importance of the feature for the Egyptians and supports the view that the concealed inner tumulus was the forerunner of the initial mastaba stage of the Step Pyramid of Djoser. Superstructures in the form of mounds were linked in Egyptian religious beliefs with the primeval mound of creation, and were desirable in helping to ensure the benefits of resurrection for the dead.

In addition to the technological innovation of the stairway entrance, the burial chamber of the tomb of Den also possessed a granite pavement, a portion of which was uncovered by Petrie. Additional use of granite and limestone was found in the south-western part of this tomb, where

58 Limestone tomb stela from the burial of a servant of King Semerkhet. The name of the owner, written Nefer, is accompanied on the stela by an ideogram of a dwarf. First Dynasty, about 2900 BC. From Abydos. H. 45 cm.

59 BELOW Excavation photograph of the remains of a human arm with linen wrappings, encircled by bracelets of gold and semi-precious stones. First Dynasty, about 3000 BC. From the tomb of King Djer at Abydos.

60 One of the pair of
tomb stelae of Queen
Merneith, from her
tomb in the royal
cemetery at Abydos
(Fig. 61). First Dynasty,
about 3000 BC.

61 BELOW
Reconstruction of the
superstructure of the
tomb of Queen
Merneith at Abydos,
showing the paired
stelae (see Fig. 60)
in the offering place.
First Dynasty, about
3000 BC.

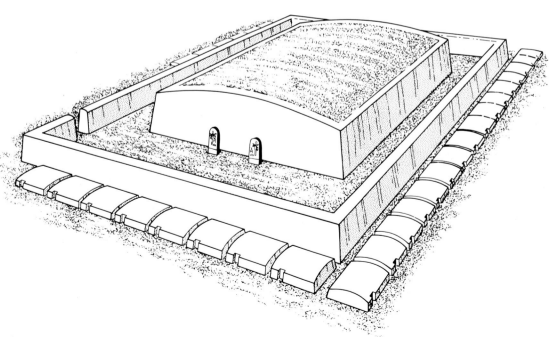

there were granite blocks to serve as the foundations of wooden roof supports. These stones lay in a small room which may have been an early example of a statue chamber, as found in tombs of the Old Kingdom. The preferred material during the First Dynasty for the embellishment of the burial chamber was not stone but wood, great quantities of which were employed for flooring the chamber, for lining the walls and for wooden shrines around the actual burial. Surprisingly large amounts of this timber were found to have survived when the tombs were excavated by Amélineau and Petrie, although in some of the tombs it had been destroyed by fire in antiquity. The wooden floor in the chamber of Anedjib was well preserved, consisting of planks about 5 centimetres in thickness, and Amélineau records the presence of the burnt remains of a wooden chamber in the tomb of Djer.

The burial place of Qa-a has recently been re-excavated by the German Archaeological Institute and new information has been gained on its history. The tomb was built in stages, with numerous additions and alterations, beginnning with a simple burial chamber with very thick walls, which were subsequently hollowed out to create storage rooms. A stairway entrance was built from the north-west, with magazines on each side of the stair at its base, an arrangement very similar to the plan of certain large contemporary tombs at Saqqara. The compartments for

62 View of the tomb of King Qa-a at Abydos, recently re-excavated by the German Archaeological Institute. The large central burial chamber is approached by the stair at the far end, and is surrounded by store-chambers and subsidiary graves. First Dynasty, about 2900 BC.

63 The tomb chamber of King Anedjib at Abydos, showing the floor of wooden planks. First Dynasty, about 3000 BC.

the subsidiary burials around the Abydos tomb were added to the existing nucleus of the brick-lined burial chamber.

The Second-Dynasty tomb of Khasekhemwy differs in design from the earlier royal tombs and had the new feature of a stone-lined burial chamber. Many rooms were included in the substructure, arranged on either side of a long passage to create a long, narrow tomb instead of the square style employed by the earlier kings. The increase in the number of rooms was almost certainly prompted by a desire to accommodate more grave-goods; contemporary tombs at Saqqara were also developing additional storage capacity in the form of rock-cut chambers on either side of a central corridor.

As mentioned above, only two kings of the Second Dynasty were buried at Abydos and others chose instead to build tombs at Saqqara. Two large substructures have been found in the area to the south of the later Step Pyramid enclosure of Djoser, but all traces of the mastaba superstructures above these tombs were swept away by building activity in the region during the Old Kingdom. Seal-impressions from the tombs bore the names of the kings Raneb, Hetepsekhemwy and Ninetjer, two of whom were presumably buried here. A granite stela with the name of Raneb is known and is suspected to have come from the Memphite region. Peribsen, however, constructed his tomb at the traditional centre of Abydos and, following his preference for the god Seth, had the animal of Seth depicted over the royal name on his tomb stelae, in place of the usual falcon of Horus. The animal of Seth, with its long snout, tall ears and forked tail, has never been satisfactorily identified, and it may have been a mythical, composite creature.

Despite repeated plundering in antiquity, not to mention the clearance and refurbishment of some of the royal tombs in connection with the Osiris cult, an astonishing quantity of the original tomb equipment survived to be discovered in the excavations of Amélineau and Petrie. Although much of the material had been smashed, the collected fragments give a good impression of the range and quantity of objects placed in the tombs. The main materials utilised in the production of grave-goods were pottery, stone, bone and ivory, glazed composition and copper. It is to be expected that the tombs would contain examples of the finest products of their day, so we may take the grave-goods as an illustration of the most advanced technology available in the First and Second Dynasties.

The vast numbers of pottery jars were primarily supplied as containers of food and drink, the Egyptian belief in provisioning the dead for the next world being already well established. Amongst the vases were imports from Syria, some examples from the tomb of Djer still containing the carbonised remains of their contents. After pottery, the most numerous items in the tombs were stone vessels in a more extensive range of shapes and materials than occurred at any other period. In addition to the cylindrical vases and bowls of calcite which constituted the most

64 Copper tools from burial equipment of the First and Second Dynasties, about 3100–2686 BC, comprising two axe-blades, a serrated knife, a chisel and two adzes. H. of tallest item 25 cm.

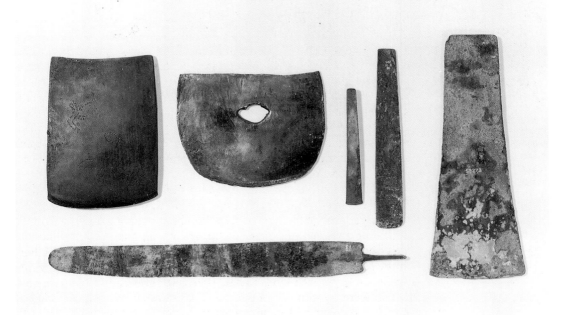

65 Two vases of dolomite limestone from the burial equipment of King Khasekhemwy. The vases have covers made of thin gold sheet, secured by fine gold wire. Second Dynasty, about 2700 BC. From Abydos. H. of taller vase 5.7 cm.

common types, there were many vessels cut from the hard stones breccia, gabbro or granite, painstakingly hollowed out with a simple crank drill tipped with stone and used with sand abrasive. There was a tendency to produce the finest vases from distinctive pieces of stone, chosen for their fine colour or natural veining, and the product might be further enhanced by the addition of gold plate over the rim or handles. Certain vessels from the Second-Dynasty tomb of Khasekhemwy had gold covers held in place by gold wire, imitating a leather or cloth cover tied with string. The styles of stone vessels in use show a development through the First and Second Dynasties, although deliberately archaising vases were occasionally produced as exotic additions to burial equipment. Under Khasekhemwy, several new styles appeared which were to form the basis of fashions in the Third Dynasty.

Copper objects, particularly tools and vessels, were fairly common in the royal tombs and occurred also in some of the subsidiary burials. The finely manufactured chisels, axes and adzes are evidence of a high degree

66 Fragment of ivory from the tomb of Den at Abydos, inscribed with the name of the king in a finely detailed *serekh* panel. First Dynasty, about 3000 BC. H. 6 cm.

67 BELOW Ivory label for a pair of sandals in the tomb equipment of King Den, decorated on the front with a scene of the king about to strike an Asiatic captive. The reverse side bears a picture of the sandals to which the label was attached. First Dynasty, about 3000 BC. From Abydos. H. 4.5 cm.

68 Bronze vessels from the tomb of Khasekhemwy at Abydos, consisting of an ewer (top) and a basin, used in washing the hands. These are the earliest examples of true bronze from Egypt. Second Dynasty, about 2700 BC. H. of basin 12 cm.

of metalworking skill, a distinct advance over the Late Predynastic Period. The technique of adding arsenic to the metal for easier casting and increased hardness of the finished tool had been perfected. Two vases from the tomb of Khasekhemwy and now in the British Museum have been found to consist of bronze, the earliest examples of this alloy so far known from Egypt. From the evidence of later texts it is known that vessels of these shapes were used in pairs for washing the hands, water being poured over the hands from the spouted vase into the open basin. The spout of this example has a double channel and was created by the process of lost-wax casting, as was the body of the vessel itself. These two vases were wrapped in linen, or perhaps contained in a linen bag before being placed in the tomb, and traces of the imprint of the cloth can be seen on the corroded surfaces. Also from the tomb of Khasekhemwy came a large number of model substitutes for implements, cut from thin copper sheet.

Small objects from the tombs included glazed composition inlays and beads, bone arrowheads and wooden or ivory furniture elements. Among the last were legs from beds carved in the style of a bull's hoof, and ivory inlay strips with diagonal patterns. That these came from boxes decorated in the palace-façade style has recently been shown by the discovery at an Early Dynastic site in the Delta of the remains of a wooden box with the panelled motif created by applied strips of the same type.

It is among the small carvings in ivory and wood that some of the most important objects from the cemetery are found, in the form of small inscribed plaques. These were normally intended to identify items of funerary equipment to which they were attached, but they also bear references to particular events in the reign of the king, and the names of certain officials who served under him. One of the finest examples is the label of Den, intended to be attached to a pair of sandals, as the representation of these on the reverse side makes clear, but inscribed on the front with a scene showing the king smiting an Asiatic and with an inscription reading: 'The first occasion of smiting the East(erners)'. Another label from the tomb of Den, this time of wood, records the king's jubilee festival with scenes of him running around the symbolic boundary markers of the land and assuming his place on the throne in a booth. This label bears the name of the official Hemaka, known from other documents of the reign at Abydos and Saqqara. These small labels are characteristic of the inscribed material which has survived from the Early Dynastic period and examples have been found at sites other than Abydos. The more elaborate labels have been discussed at length, chiefly because our knowledge of the language of this period is limited and as a consequence different interpretations of the inscriptions are possible. Some of the labels are much simpler, bearing only a representation of the object to which they were attached, such as a wooden plaque from the tomb of Djer with an incised illustration of a gaming-piece. More informative versions of this kind of document are the small labels from the palace-façade mastaba of Naqada, which provide a picture of the necklace to which they were attached and numerals recording the number of beads on the object. On some of the labels primitive buildings are shown, usually shrines constructed of reeds, but these may be archaising illustrations showing the shrines in their prototype forms instead of as they may have appeared in the early dynasties. One of the most important inscriptions of this kind is a label of Aha from Abydos with a representation of a shrine of the goddess Neith.

The interest generated by the brief texts on small ivory and wooden labels is in part due to the lack of more substantial inscriptions from the period. Most of the recorded texts come from inscribed stone vases, cylinder seals or seal-impressions on clay jar-stoppers, none of which are good media for extensive inscriptions. There are also the Abydos royal

69 The name of a vineyard of King Semerkhet, inscribed on a fragment from a pottery wine-jar. First Dynasty, about 2900 BC. From Abydos. H. 33 cm.

and private tomb stelae, but the inscriptions on these are for the most part limited to names until very late in the First Dynasty, when the stelae of two officials from the reign of Qa-a also include their titles. Officials' names are often recorded on the clay seal-impressions which have been found in many Early Dynastic tombs. Large clay seals were placed over the lids of wine-jars, serving to hold the lid in place and providing a location for the seal-impression of the official responsible for supervising the preparation of this material for the tomb. The seals are either conical or take the form of a flattened hemisphere; they were normally impressed repeatedly, with two crossing inscriptions over the top of the seal and another around the sides near the base. In the case of wine-jars, a reference to the area of production is often included in the inscription. In addition, the name of the vineyard might also be incised on the pottery jar itself: several examples of such inscribed jars were found in the tomb of Semerkhet at Abydos.

The cemeteries of Saqqara, Tarkhan and others

In the excavations carried out by W.B. Emery between 1936 and 1956, a series of great palace-façade mastaba tombs of the First Dynasty was found along the eastern edge of the escarpment at north Saqqara. The tombs were architecturally sophisticated and contained remnants of fine grave-goods, with objects in ivory, metal and glazed composition of similar quality to those from the royal tombs of Abydos. Emery put

70 Plan and section of tomb 3504 at Saqqara, a fine example of the palace-façade mastaba tombs belonging to high officials of the First Dynasty.

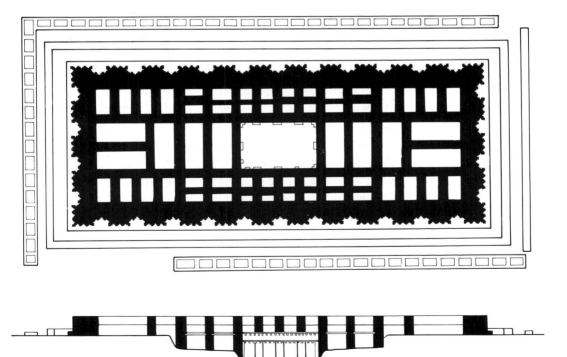

71 Limestone stela of
the official Merka, from
his tomb at Saqqara.
One of the small
number of texts of any
length from the First
Dynasty, it contains a
list of Merka's titles.
About 2900 BC.

forward a view that certain of these Saqqara tombs were those of the First-Dynasty kings themselves, reclassifying their southern tombs as cenotaphs. This opinion was based essentially on the size of the Saqqara mastabas, which considerably exceeded that of the Abydos tombs, although the presence of the funerary enclosures at Abydos was not taken into account. In recent years the balance of discussion on this topic has swung back in favour of Abydos being the true burial place of the First-Dynasty rulers and the Saqqara tombs being those of high officials. New evidence from Abydos supports this view, particularly the natural evolution of the royal cemetery at Umm el-Qaab from the Predynastic Cemetery U, and the fact that the tomb of Qa-a shows signs of multiple building phases. One serious problem with the theory that the Saqqara tombs were royal monuments was the fact that the number of tombs at the site considerably exceeded the number of kings. Although the tombs contained seal-impressions with the names of the First-Dynasty kings, the seal of the same ruler might occur in several mastabas, suggesting that they were in fact monuments which happened to be constructed during a particular reign. These seals also bore the names of the high officials who were probably the true owners of the tombs, and it is interesting that some of these functionaries are known from inscriptions found at Abydos. Their importance for the administration of the country is reflected in the wealth of their burials, as demonstrated by the remains of the grave-goods and the monumental nature of the tombs themselves.

In the case of one of the tombs the ownership is confirmed by the presence of a limestone stela which was once fixed in a recess near the south end of the east face, a location later to become the traditional offering point. This stela bore the name of the priestly official Merka, who served under King Qa-a late in the First Dynasty. The style of this stela, which includes a relief seated figure of the owner and a list of his titles, anticipates the decorated wooden panels of the Third-Dynasty tomb of Hesyra. It is interesting that already in the First Dynasty we find prominence given to the enumeration of titles, which was to become one of the most enduring features of Egyptian biographical and funerary texts in later periods. The large tomb associated with the stela of Merka, numbered 3505, possessed a remarkable funerary chapel of several rooms at the north end of the superstructure; in this were found the remains of two large wooden figures, presumably cult-statues of Merka.

The tombs of Saqqara exhibit a steady development from the earliest, dated to the reign of Aha, down to the end of the First Dynasty. At the beginning of the sequence there was no entrance stair to the burial chamber, which was sunk into the surface of the desert under the middle of the superstructure and roofed with wood. As at Abydos, the stairway entrance first appears in the tombs from the time of Den and is accompanied by the introduction of deeper burial chambers. The stair was closed by the use of slabs of limestone lowered on ropes and engaged in recesses in the sides of the passage; this system of so-called 'portcullis-blocks' was refined in the Old Kingdom and used extensively in the pyramids. In the early tombs, only the burial chamber and the rooms

immediately around it were sunk below ground level, and additional storage space for grave-goods was provided in magazines in the upper part of the superstructure. Gradually, more of these stores were transferred to the substructure of the tombs and by the end of the First Dynasty the mastaba was a solid mass of brick and gravel fill. The nature of the limestone plateau at Saqqara afforded a good medium for underground tunnelling, and in the large tomb 3035, which belonged to an official of King Den named Hemaka, rock-cut storerooms were cut around a conventional wooden-roofed burial chamber. In the reign of Qa-a, the entrance stair was arranged to enter directly into a substructure hollowed out of the rock. The absence of this development in the royal tombs of Abydos was due to the lack of good-quality rock strata at a high level in the desert. The availability of good limestone in the Memphite region made that area the focal point for early developments in stoneworking, and limestone was employed in tomb chambers of the First Dynasty at Helwan, east of Memphis.

Together with the gradual expansion of the underground portions of the Saqqara tombs and the consequent reduction of the number of chambers in the superstructure, palace-façade panelling of the brickwork became less common, and after the end of the First Dynasty appeared only in isolated revivals, such as the Third-Dynasty mastaba of Hesyra. It was replaced by tombs with two simple recesses, one at each end of the east face, the southern niche serving as the principal offering place. This location had already been selected as the significant point for

72 OPPOSITE Interior of the burial chamber of tomb 3500 at Saqqara, showing the descending stairway closed by 'portcullis-slabs' of limestone. First Dynasty, about 2900 BC.

73 Ivory figure of a lion, a particularly fine example of the kind used as gaming pieces and found among the funerary equipment of Early Dynastic tombs. Probably First Dynasty, about 3100–2890 BC. H. 2.1 cm.

74 Subsidiary graves of servants around the large tomb 3500 at Saqqara. Each servant burial was covered by a small mastaba superstructure over a brick-vaulted chamber. First Dynasty, about 2900 BC.

offerings prior to the disappearance of the palace-façade, as shown by the position of the stela of Merka, mentioned above, in one of the recesses of a panelled superstructure close to the south end of the east face. A palace-façade mastaba is also known from an extensive First-Dynasty cemetery at Tarkhan with one recess in the same position accorded special significance by the presence of a wooden floor. The location of the offering recess at this early period established a rule which was to determine the position of the more elaborate chapels of tombs throughout the Old Kingdom, and which was also responsible for the similar location of the entrance to the enclosure of the Step Pyramid of Djoser. Another significant link between the First-Dynasty mastabas of Saqqara and the development of the Step Pyramid was the presence of brick-cased tumuli over the burial-pits of certain tombs, hidden within the palace-façade superstructure. As more fully described in Chapter 5 below, some have seen the pyramid in its enclosure as a greatly enlarged version of the earlier tumulus inside a panelled mastaba.

The Saqqara tombs of the First Dynasty were rich in funerary furniture. Like the royal tombs at Abydos, the burial chambers were floored with wood and in one case the walls were lined with the same material, embellished with gold strips. Surviving objects from the burial equipment were found in the burial chambers and in the storage magazines, including some of the finest Early Dynastic antiquities to have come to light. Fine stone vases of exotic and unusual forms supplemented the mass of more standard types; a collection of copper vessels and tools was found in a tomb from the reign of Djer; a gaming-board and associated pieces came from a mastaba dated to Djet, and an ebony box containing a roll of uninscribed papyrus from the tomb of Hemaka. The last is the earliest known example of papyrus and its presence may indicate that this writing medium was already in use in the First Dynasty.

Like the royal tombs of Abydos, some of the great mastabas of the First-Dynasty officials at Saqqara were surrounded by subsidiary graves, some of which were marked by rough limestone stelae identifying the occupants. The number of these burials was far smaller than recorded at the kings' tombs, although the arrangement of the graves was similar to those at Abydos, placed in brick-lined pits or trenches around the main tomb. In certain cases the superstructures of the subsidiary graves had survived to some height, providing some firm information on the visible parts of the graves above ground level which was not obtained at Abydos owing to the greater destruction of the site. Each grave was covered by a small brick mastaba, convex at the top and with a small offering niche in one side. The grave-pit below this mastaba was either roofed with wood, or, in the case of the subsidiary burials around the the large tomb 3500 of the reign of Qa-a, with a brick vault, the earliest known. These primitive vaults had been constructed of rings of mud brick which inclined towards one end of the roof to aid cohesion between one course and the next. This method of construction continued in use thoughout the history of Egyptian civilisation and down to fairly recent times, an illustration of the longevity of early technical innovations in Egyptian culture.

Saqqara was not the only site at which large tombs of the First Dynasty occurred: examples are also known from Giza and Tarkhan, in addition to the great mastaba at Naqada (see above, p.60). Medium-size and small tombs of the dynasty have been found throughout the country and, through their architecture and grave-goods, they provide clear evidence of political stability which encouraged trade and allowed for increasing wealth. After the close of the Second Dynasty the importance of Abydos diminished as the site was abandoned as a royal cemetery in favour of Saqqara, close to the capital at Memphis. The importance of Abydos during the first two dynasties was an effect of the Upper Egyptian origin of the kings, but with the whole land unified and secure the ties to the old centres of the south were gradually lessened.

5

Stability and formal style in the Early Old Kingdom

The dramatic advances in political organisation, technology and wealth made during the Early Dynastic Period established Egypt as a major power, trading with the countries of the Near East, exercising control over the Nubian province and exploiting both Nubia and Sinai for their mineral resources. That the state should have achieved such prominence through the development of highly central-ised power in a relatively short time is remarkable, as was the rate of technical progress and artistic accomplishment. It is at the beginning of the Third Dynasty (about 2686 BC) that we see a major result of the application of new skills, in the construction of the Step Pyramid of King Djoser at Saqqara. This monument represents the first attempt of the Egyptians to build entirely in stone; previously they had constructed only to a limited extent in this material, as, for example, in the tomb of Khasekhemwy at Abydos with its stone-lined chamber. Also at Abydos, the floor of the First-Dynasty tomb of Den had been paved with granite, showing early competence in the dressing of hard stone, but these elements of the Abydos tombs were always ancillary to the main mud-brick fabric of the buildings. The Step Pyramid is a monument of an entirely different scale, embodying not only the ability to quarry, transport and place vast numbers of stone blocks, but also elegant design features in the complex surrounding the pyramid, with its limestone columns based on plant prototypes. To a large extent the ability of the builders to create the pyramid complex was based on the long-estab-lished experience which had been gained in the working of stone during the early dynasties, by the creation of thousands of stone vessels in hard materials. Added to this skill was that of cutting limestone, acquired as part of the process of excavating tomb chambers in the rock. This practice had been applied to the Saqqara necropolis, in particular, from the middle of the First Dynasty.

The Step Pyramid of Djoser and its surrounding complex of buildings display interesting links with both the preceding early dynasties and the apogee of the pyramid age in the succeeding Fourth Dynasty. The design of the enclosing wall of the complex reproduces the appearance of the First-Dynasty tombs at Saqqara and elsewhere, with the characteristic

panelled appearance known as 'palace-façade'. As explained previously, this panelling was imitative of primitive architectural structures made of bundles of reeds bound together, and despite the formalised version of the panels found in mud-brick mastabas or in the enclosure wall of the Step Pyramid itself, the Egyptians were fully aware of the origin of the design. This fact is clearly demonstrated in the underground chambers of the Step Pyramid, in which the sides of the passages were embellished with the same palace-façade motif, reproduced in blue-green tiles inlaid into the limestone walls in a realistic representation of a primitive screen of reed-matting. The same design also occurs in the corridors below the so-called South Tomb, a dummy burial place under the south wall of the enclosure, duplicating the chambers below the pyramid itself.

In both sets of passages the palace-façade decoration of the walls is further enhanced by the inclusion of low-relief carvings at the back of each recess, showing the king engaged in episodes from the jubilee festival. The style and content of these reliefs again show links with the First Dynasty: a depiction of the king performing part of the jubilee ritual by running around boundary markers is similar to the representation of King Den on the wooden label from his tomb. In fact, this scene became adopted as part of the standard repertoire of later temple reliefs, and examples are found at all periods down to Roman times. The repetition of

75 The Step Pyramid of Djoser at Saqqara, seen from the south. Third Dynasty, about 2680 BC.

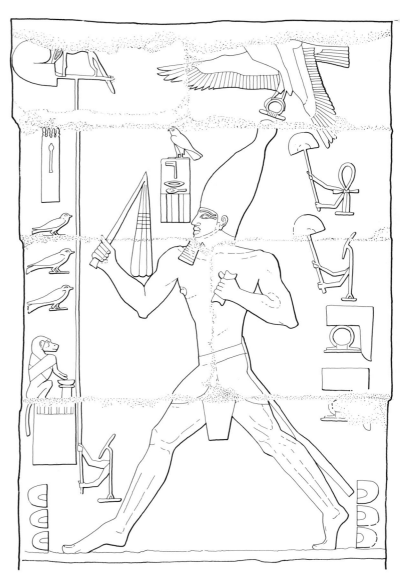

76 King Djoser performing the ritual of running around the boundary markers in the jubilee festival, signifying his authority over the land. From a relief below the Step Pyramid at Saqqara. Third Dynasty, about 2680 BC.

designs and motifs first established in the early dynasties throughout the later history of Egypt is a characteristic of the civilisation, and was not accidental but part of a conscious desire by the Egyptians to maintain continuity with their own past. From the perspective of the ancient Egyptians, advancement was always regarded as being best achieved by maintaining the existing order. The sandstone relief of King Sanakht, possibly the successor of Djoser, striking an Asiatic tribesman is another example of the same process, since the motif duplicates that on the ivory label of Den. A slightly different prototype of this image may be seen on the ceremonial slate palette of Narmer in the Egyptian Museum, Cairo, but the scene very quickly became fixed in a standard mode. The Sanakht

relief came from Wadi Maghara in Sinai, where very similar scenes existed showing Djoser and Sekhemkhet with defeated captives.

The Step Pyramid, as one might expect for an experimental structure in a new material, was built in a series of stages, beginning as a square mastaba tomb. The incorporation of a mastaba into the structure very probably had a ritual significance as the traditional royal tomb superstructure, used above the burial chambers of the First-Dynasty tombs at Abydos. Possibly the surrounding enclosure is the equivalent of the large mud-brick funerary enclosures at Abydos, but placed around the grave superstructure to form a single unit instead of at a distance as in the earlier arrangement. The same combination of the two elements of the Abydos tombs has been noted in the case of the great First-Dynasty mastaba tombs of officials at Saqqara, the design of which, with a tumulus inside a panelled façade, may represent a stage in the evolution of the Step Pyramid. Although the brick-cased tumulus over the burial-pit was only clearly evident in two of the Saqqara tombs, numbers 3507 and 3038, the excavator believed that it might have been a common feature of all the tombs. In tomb 3507, dating from the early First Dynasty, the tumulus was a simple affair of rubble with sloping sides, cased with mud brick. The later mastaba 3038, which may have

77 Sandstone relief fragment showing King Sanakht with a foreign captive. Third Dynasty, about 2680 BC. From Wadi Maghara in Sinai. H. 33 cm.

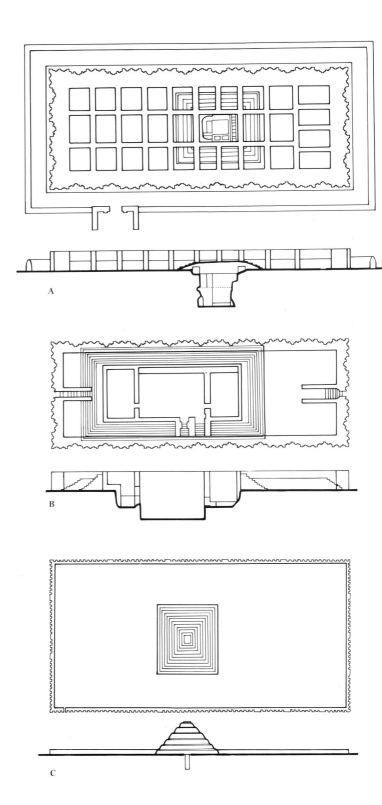

78 The possible
evolution of the step
pyramid from the
primitive tumulus over
the burial pit of First-
Dynasty tombs,
showing (A) a panelled
mastaba with an
internal simple
tumulus, (B) a similar
mastaba containing a
stepped tumulus, and
(c) the step pyramid
within its panelled
enclosure wall.

belonged to an official of King Anedjib named Nebitka, possessed a stepped internal mound, providing an even closer link with the Step Pyramid.

The initial stone mastaba of the Step Pyramid was enlarged before the upper steps of the monument were built above it, first as a pyramid of four steps, later increased to six. In its final stage, the pyramid rose to a height of about 60 metres. The exterior masonry of each phase consisted of a casing of finely dressed limestone to cover the rougher internal construction. In a link with earlier mud-brick building, beams of timber were inserted into the structure in an attempt to improve stability, and the stones of the core were laid in alternate header and stretcher courses. Access to the burial chamber, constructed at the foot of a deep pit in the rock under the pyramid, was originally intended to be gained by means of an open trench from the north, but this was covered by the enlargement of the building and a tunnel was cut instead. Also on the north of the pyramid was the mortuary temple for the cult of the dead king, a statue of whom was placed in a nearby chamber. In addition to the king's name, the pedestal of the statue bore the name of the chief minister of the reign, Imhotep, regarded as the architect of the royal tomb and deified in later periods as a god of healing.

Very little remains of this temple, but the other buildings of the complex, to the east of the pyramid, had survived sufficiently for substantial reconstruction to be carried out. These structures were chiefly dummies, consisting of façades with solid rubble interiors, and were provided for ritual purposes. The royal jubilee or *Sed*-festival has already been mentioned in connection with the reliefs below the pyramid, and many of the buildings in the enclosure were associated with this ritual. In the great courtyard to the south of the pyramid stood two pairs of stone boundary markers – built remains of the features depicted on the reliefs – around which the king was supposed to run. Other buildings in the complex were probably intended to represent sanctuaries from different parts of Egypt, particularly since the reliefs in the pyramid chambers include depictions of such shrines. The architectural style of these buildings is surprisingly sophisticated, with exquisitely carved engaged columns in the form of papyrus stems or clusters of reeds. Fluted columns also occur, the first examples of a type which was to reappear in the architecture of the Middle and New Kingdoms.

The burial chamber of the king was built of granite and entered only from the top, through a narrow aperture in the roof which was sealed by a granite plug. Of the burial there remained only a linen-wrapped foot, possibly from the original interment. Although the king is generally referred to by the name Djoser, the evidence for this name comes only from later records; all the contemporary inscriptions in the pyramid complex and elsewhere use the Horus-name Netjerikhet, written in the *serekh*-panel as was usual practice during the Early Dynastic Period. Numerous inscriptions were recovered from underground galleries beneath the pyramid or below other parts of the complex, cut on some of the thousands of stone vessels found during the exploration of the passages. The texts possess very much of the archaic character familiar from inscriptions found in the Abydos tombs, and in certain cases they are quite similar, giving the names of officials and of particular buildings or localities. Strangely, none of the inscribed stone vessels bore the Horus-name Netjerikhet, but the names of several First- and Second-Dynasty kings occurred, suggesting that the burial equipment had been supplemented with a large number of old vases. It is possible that some of the galleries below the Djoser complex, particularly those on the west of the pyramid, had originally formed the substructures of large Second-Dynasty tombs cleared away by Djoser. This possibility is supported by the presence at Saqqara of the tombs of two kings of the Second Dynasty, situated just south of the Step Pyramid enclosure (see above, p.84). If earlier tombs were removed to clear the site for the construction of the pyramid, some of the reused funerary equipment could have been collected from their substructures. It seems that even at this early stage in Egyptian history the kings were not averse to removing the funerary monuments of their predecessors for pragmatic reasons.

The political history of the Third Dynasty is far from clear, despite the substantial monuments which remain from the period. To the west of the Step Pyramid at Saqqara are the unexcavated remains of two other large enclosures, probably unfinished step pyramid complexes of some of Djoser's successors. The names of Netjerikhet (Djoser) and Sanakht occur on mud seal-impressions from two huge brick mastaba tombs at Beit Khallaf near Abydos, apparently the burial places of important officials of the Third Dynasty. These tombs, excavated by John Garstang in 1900, contain the earliest examples of the true arch used in Egyptian architecture. More recent excavations have produced inscriptions of Sanakht and Netjerikhet from the early town at Elephantine.

79 Plan of the underground galleries south of the funerary complex of King Djoser at Saqqara. The galleries probably date from the Second Dynasty, about 2890–2686 BC.

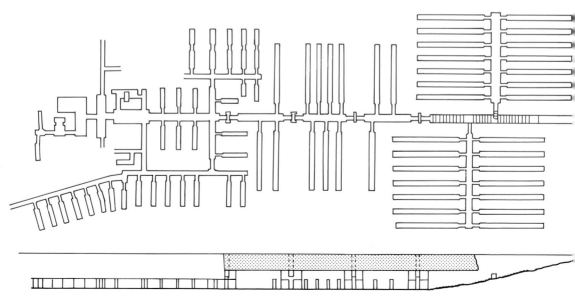

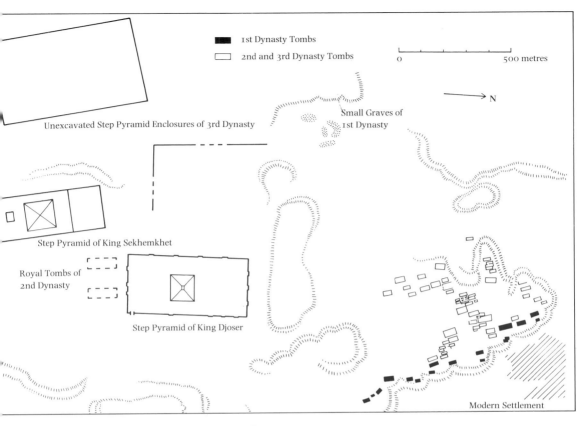

80 Map of the Early
Dynastic monuments
of Saqqara.

Another step pyramid of the dynasty is known, again at Saqqara, a short distance to the south-west of the Djoser pyramid. The builder of this complex is known to have been King Sekhemkhet, who evidently died while his tomb was still under construction, for the building was left in an incomplete state. It is not known what happened to his body: when the sarcophagus in the burial chamber below the pyramid was opened in 1955, it proved to be empty. This pyramid was surrounded by a panelled enclosure, inside which, to the south of the pyramid, was a mastaba tomb analogous to the 'South Tomb' of Djoser. The purpose of these additional tombs is still unclear, but they are doubtless the antecedents of the enigmatic subsidiary pyramids found to the south or south-east of the pyramid tombs of the Fourth Dynasty and later. Some jewellery was found in the descending passage of the Sekhemkhet pyramid and a quantity of stone vases was recovered from the underground passages. Apart from this pyramid, Sekhemkhet is only known from a rock inscription in Sinai.

To the north of the Step Pyramid of Djoser is an extensive high plateau, the northern part of which was used in the Third Dynasty for the construction of private tombs in mastaba form. The eastern part of the same region had been occupied with tombs of the First and Second Dynasties, including the fine palace-façade mastabas of the First-Dynasty officials. In the Third-Dynasty part of the necropolis there were rows of large brick tombs of wealthy individuals with later, smaller tombs clustered around them. Few of the tombs had palace-façade panelling, this fashion having been replaced by the custom of providing two simple recesses in the east face of the superstructure, which was otherwise plain white-plastered brickwork. The southern recess was the larger of the two and was a simple offering-chapel, where food and drink could be presented for the benefit of the deceased. Originally the recess contained an inscribed panel of stone or wood giving the name and titles of the tomb owner, together with a relief showing a formal scene of the deceased seated before a table of offerings. A good example of a stone panel of this type is the limestone slab of Rahotep, which comes from his brick mastaba tomb at Meidum; a simpler version is exemplified by a slab from the tomb of Hezi, in the British Museum.

The majority of the Third-Dynasty tombs in the Saqqara cemetery retained no clue as to the identities of their owners owing to the fact that they had been extensively plundered, but one large mastaba was found to contain a remarkable series of inscribed wooden panels. This tomb, belonging to an individual named Hesyra, was unusual in retaining the old palace-façade motif along its eastern face, protected by a wall so that the decorative design was enclosed by a narrow corridor. Sheltered from the weather, the panelled face had survived with remains of the original painted detail and the carved wooden panels at the rear of the main recesses of the façade. The panels bear reliefs of Hesyra with inscriptions recording his titles, the disposition of the hieroglyphs exhibiting the archaic feature of loose grouping of the signs without dividing lines between the columns, but the quality with which the individual hieroglyphs are cut is excellent. The painted decoration on the recessed wall of the tomb consisted of colourful patterns to imitate the appearance of reed-matting screens, in the same style as the designs on the First-Dynasty tombs of Saqqara. More informative paintings were preserved on the opposite wall, that is the interior east side of the corridor, where detailed representations of items from the funerary furniture had been executed. These fine illustrations showed beds, chairs and stools, chests and boxes, some of the latter with their contents – tools, razors, jars of oils and games – precisely depicted. The paintings were accompanied by inscriptions which identified the objects, and mark the earliest large-scale identification list of funerary equipment to have survived, the beginning of a custom which appeared regularly in later periods, for example in the decoration of Middle Kingdom coffins.

Such funerary equipment as survived the repeated plundering of the underground chambers of the tomb lay scattered in fragments and consisted only of those items considered not worth removing, for the most part broken stone and pottery vases. A clay seal-impression with the *serekh* of Netjerikhet provided evidence to date the tomb to the time of Djoser. The tomb of Hesyra had been one of the richest Third-Dynasty mastabas in the Saqqara necropolis and the chance preservation of its fine painted corridor-chapel was most fortunate. Other tombs of similar

81 Wooden panel from the tomb of Hesyra at Saqqara, with a relief showing the owner. The arrangement of the hieroglyphs in vertical columns without dividing lines is characteristic of the period. Third Dynasty, about 2650 BC. H. 115 cm. Cairo, Egyptian Museum.

size and date, such as the anonymous mastaba 3518 excavated by the Egypt Exploration Society, have yielded less informative material.

Saqqara was undoubtedly the most important of the Third-Dynasty cemeteries and it retained its significance throughout the Old Kingdom and into later periods. Tombs from the Third Dynasty also occur at many sites along the length of the Nile Valley and range from poor graves to substantial funerary monuments of mud brick. In addition to the great mastaba tombs of Beit Khallaf, mentioned above, there was a very large Third-Dynasty tomb at Giza which, like the tomb of Hesyra, possessed the archaic feature of palace-façade recessing. This extended around all sides of the tomb, but for some reason it had been hidden by a brick wall constructed in a second building phase around the superstructure. A notable difference between the tombs of the period in the Memphite region and those in Upper Egypt was the form of the descent to the burial chamber, which in the north took the form of a vertical pit but at southern sites was built as a sloping stairway.

The pattern established by Djoser of constructing tombs in the form of step pyramids was maintained to the end of the Third Dynasty and into the beginning of the Fourth. A very ruined pyramid at Zawiyet el-Aryan may have belonged to a king with the Horus-name Khaba, found inscribed on stone vessels in mastaba tombs near the pyramid. But the most significant monument in the development of the Old Kingdom royal tomb is the pyramid at Meidum, which was initially constructed in stepped form but later altered into the first true pyramid. As in the pyramid of Djoser, several phases of building were involved. First, a step pyramid with seven steps was built, but then enlarged to eight steps. Owing to the later partial destruction of the monument, some of the

82 OPPOSITE The pyramid of Meidum viewed from the east, along the line of its associated causeway. Fourth Dynasty, about 2600 BC.

83 Section of the pyramid of Meidum, showing the two successive stepped phases and the final true pyramid form.

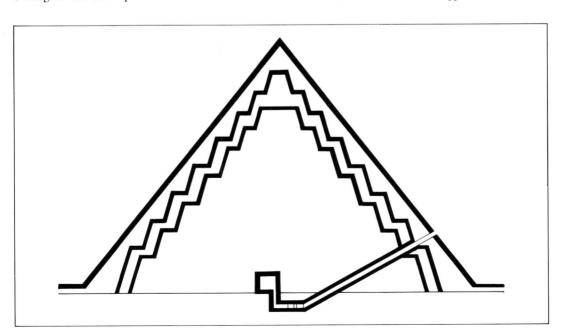

84 Fragment of plaster wall-painting from the tomb of Itet at Meidum, showing a man feeding an antelope. Fourth Dynasty, about 2600 BC. H. 46 cm.

casings of the earlier phase have been revealed, providing useful information on its internal structure and building history. The enlarged step pyramid was finally converted to a true pyramidal shape by the addition of masonry to fill in the steps. Other important innovations appear at Meidum: for the first time the mortuary temple was built against the east face of the structure instead of at the north, and a causeway leading to a valley temple was provided, where the body of the king would arrive at the funerary complex. These elements remained standard in all the later pyramids, the temples of which became increasingly lavish, with much use of hard stones for pavements and columns.

It would seem that the increasing importance of solar worship was responsible for the new location of the temples on the east of the pyramid. The mortuary temple of the Meidum pyramid is simple in the extreme, consisting of a single roofed chamber with an open court beyond, in which stand two limestone stelae, larger versions of the paired stelae which had been set up at the royal tombs of the First Dynasty. Unfortunately, the stelae at Meidum were never inscribed and the identity of the owner is open to dispute. In the New Kingdom, visitors to the small temple believed the pyramid had belonged to Sneferu, first king of the Fourth Dynasty, and they left evidence of their views in graffiti on the walls. The only difficulty with this suggestion lies in the fact that Sneferu is known to have built two other large pyramids at Dahshur and a small one at Seila, and the idea of a king building four such monuments in a single reign has been too much for some scholars to accept. Consequently, the stepped phase of the Meidum pyramid has been conveniently ascribed to Huni, last king of the Third Dynasty, about whom we know nothing. Whatever the truth, the Meidum pyramid was not used for a burial and the burial chamber was left incomplete.

To the north of the pyramid lay a number of very large mastabas, including the tomb of Rahotep from which came the fine inscribed panel with a figure of the owner and a list of offerings. This tomb consisted of a mud-brick casing around a core of stone rubble; the external walls were covered with white plaster, and were plain except around the chapel at the south end of the east face, where palace-façade recesses occurred. From another tomb in the same cemetery came fragments of painted wall-plaster showing the feeding of an antelope and hunters with a duck. In addition to the increasingly competent decoration of tomb chapels, the tombs of Meidum contained some very fine examples of early tomb sculptures, sealed into the body of the mastaba to guarantee a functioning home for the spirit of the owner, through which the benefit of food offerings could be received. The famous statues of Rahotep and Nefert in the Egyptian Museum, Cairo, show that the formal style normally associated with Egyptian sculpture had been achieved by the beginning of the Fourth Dynasty. Relics of the formative stage which led to such works are illustrated by slightly earlier sculptures such as that of Ankhwa in the British Museum, which exhibits the early feature of a stool with hollowed sides. Ankhwa is shown with some individuality, holding an adze appropriate to his trade as a shipbuilder.

85 A man holding a duck. Fragment of plaster wall-painting from the tomb of Itet at Meidum. Fourth Dynasty, about 2600 BC. L. 59 cm.

86 Limestone slab from the tomb of Rahotep, carved with a scene showing the deceased seated before a table of offerings. Fourth Dynasty, about 2600 BC. From Meidum. H. 79 cm.

87 OPPOSITE Limestone block from the tomb of Rahotep, carved with part of a list of funerary equipment, naming fifteen items of furniture (top) and three of the sacred oils (lower edge). Fourth Dynasty, about 2600 BC. H. 105 cm.

The two pyramids of Sneferu at Dahshur illustrate the rapid progress in constructional ability which had taken place since the building of Djoser's pyramid. Large blocks of limestone were used with confidence, the interior chambers and passages were expertly assembled, and among the associated temples were grand structures with extensive decoration in relief. Of the two pyramids, the southern or Bent Pyramid was the earlier and its lower part was formed of courses of masonry which tilt downwards, an old technique of the Third Dynasty. For the higher courses a new system of laying the blocks horizontally was introduced, a practice followed in the northern pyramid at Dahshur. The Bent Pyramid underwent changes in design which gave rise to its altered angle of slope. Apparently there were serious weaknesses in the structure which prompted emergency remedial measures, although the problem was never properly solved since the cause lay in the unsuitable nature of the desert surface on which the pyramid was built. The interior of the pyramid is unusual in having an entrance from the west in addition to one from the north side, the standard location of the entrances to all other Old Kingdom pyramids. Corbelled roofs were employed in the

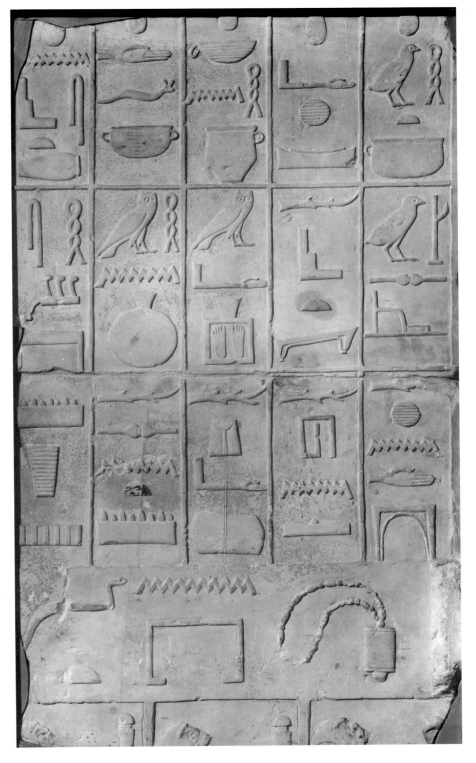

88 Granite statue of Ankhwa the shipbuilder, shown holding a carpenter's adze. Third Dynasty, about 2650 BC. H. 64 cm.

89 OPPOSITE Limestone stela inscribed with the names of King Sneferu, from the temple of the Bent Pyramid at Dahshur. Note the traditional panelled motif at the base of the *serekh*. Fourth Dynasty, about 2600 BC.

internal chambers, as in the pyramid of Meidum, but on a much grander scale. Although the mortuary temple of the Bent Pyramid was quite a small structure, similar to that at Meidum, the valley temple was an impressive monument embellished with reliefs and statues of the king.

The northern pyramid of Sneferu at Dahshur is free from the overt alterations in design seen at Meidum and in the Bent Pyramid. This monument is not much inferior in volume to that of his son and successor, Khufu, builder of the Great Pyramid at Giza. It contains three corbelled chambers, arranged in a series at the end of a long descending entrance passage, the last of which is positioned at a high level and was probably intended to serve as the burial chamber. Since this pyramid is the latest of those attributed to Sneferu, it was probably his final resting place. The adjacent mortuary temple was decorated with large reliefs depicting the king in the attire of the royal jubilee festival.

The Great Pyramid of Khufu at Giza has been described and discussed more than any other monument of ancient Egypt; it is remarkable not only for its sheer size – it rises 146 metres – but for the extreme accuracy of its orientation to the cardinal points. Great precision was also achieved in the placing of the casing blocks, with the result that extremely fine joins were made in spite of the difficulty of manoeuvring the sixteen-ton stones into position. The fragments of two casing stones in the British Museum retain portions of the sloping face of the pyramid; originally the whole surface of the monument was clad with this fine limestone. Granite from Aswan was used on a large scale inside the pyramid for the construction of the passages and chambers. Three changes of plan are evident in the construction, as the position of the burial chamber was altered from a point in the bedrock under the pyramid to a location in the interior masonry. These changes were the cause of a particular problem concerning the sealing of the tomb, because the fact that the burial chamber was located at the top of an ascending passage meant that the usual process of lowering plug-blocks into the corridor could only be accomplished from inside. As a result, the internal architecture was extensively modified to allow space for the blocking stones and for the tackle to move them into place, and also to provide a rough exit passage for the workmen.

Hardly anything remains of the mortuary temple of Khufu to the east of the pyramid apart from some areas of the basalt pavement, although the plan of the building has been recovered through excavation. The walls of the temple and also, probably, of the causeway were decorated. In recent years some parts of the valley temple have been found at the edge of the plateau, buried in the settlement at Nazlet es-Samman. The pyramids and their temples were used as quarries in later periods, and stones may have been removed to distant sites. This process was already established in Pharaonic times, and a red granite slab in the British Museum collection with the Horus-name of Khufu, written Medjedu, was probably removed from the pyramid temples in the Twenty-Second Dynasty for use in construction work at Bubastis in the Delta.

The building of the Great Pyramid in about 2580 BC is an appropriate

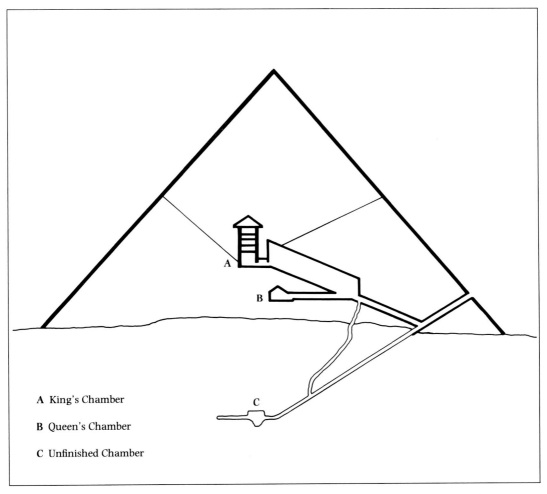

A King's Chamber

B Queen's Chamber

C Unfinished Chamber

point at which to end an account of the early history of Egypt, since, more than any other monument, it is an expression of the desire for permanence which came to be so important in ancient Egyptian thought and which did much to halt the experimentation of the early dynasties. By the Old Kingdom the belief that progress was equal to maintenance of the traditional order had already been established, dampening innovation and focusing instead on the creation of monuments intended to prolong the status quo. It was this view which was responsible for the character of ancient Egyptian civilisation, in which all that was traditional was to be reproduced over the centuries according to the original divinely inspired pattern. The fact that Egyptian monuments of widely differing dates are so instantly recognisable as products of ancient Egypt is a result of this attitude. The forms, symbols and building designs copied down the ages had their origin in the formative period of the early dynasties, probably the most innovative stage in the history of the whole civilisation, about which there remains so much to discover.

90 Section of the pyramid of Khufu at Giza. Fourth Dynasty, about 2580 BC.

91 The pyramid of
Khufu at Giza, from the
west. Fourth Dynasty,
about 2580 BC.

Further Reading

ADAMS, B., *Predynastic Egypt*, Aylesbury, 1988.

EMERY, W.B., *Archaic Egypt*, Harmondsworth, 1961.

HOFFMAN, M.A., *Egypt before the Pharaohs*, London, 1980.

LAUER, J.P., *Saqqara, Royal Cemetery of Memphis*, London, 1976.

RICE, M., *Egypt's Making*, London, 1990.

TRIGGER, B.G., Kemp, B.J., O'Connor, D., and Lloyd, A.B. (eds), *Ancient Egypt: A Social History*, Cambridge, 1983.

WATSON, P., *Egyptian Pyramids and Mastaba Tombs*, Aylesbury, 1987.

List of Illustrations

Accession numbers of objects in the Department of Egyptian Antiquities, British Museum, are prefixed EA.

22 Pottery vase with painted decoration.
   EA 35502
23 The 'Painted Tomb' at Hierakonpolis.
   Photo Egypt Exploration Society
24 Siltstone palette with two birds' heads.
   EA 32503
25 Red breccia vessel in the shape of a frog.
   EA 65240
26 Flint knife with carved ivory handle.
   EA 68512
27 Pressure-flaked flint knives.
   From top: EA 59235, 29286
28 Basalt tubular vase.
   EA 29923
29 Diadem.
   EA 37532
30 Cylindrical vase inscribed with the name of Ka.
   EA 35508
31 Copper harpoon blade.
   EA 49007
32 Ceremonial palette of King Narmer.
   Egyptian Museum, Cairo
33 'Towns' palette.
   Egyptian Museum, Cairo
34, 35 'Battlefield' palette.
   EA 20971
36 Relief on mace-head of King Scorpion.
   Drawing by Richard Parkinson after Marian Cox
37 'Hunters' palette.
   EA 20970
38 Palace-façade brickwork.
   Drawing by Christine Barratt after W.B. Emery
39 *Serekh* with the name Aha.
   EA 38010
40 Part of the superstructure of the tomb of Queen Neithhotep, Naqada.
   Drawing by Christine Barratt after J. de Morgan
41 Ivory label from the tomb of Queen Neithhotep, Naqada.
   EA 55588
42 Inscription on ivory label from the tomb of Queen Neithhotep, Naqada.
   Drawing by Richard Parkinson
43 Seal-impression with the names of First-Dynasty rulers.
   Drawing by Christine Barratt after G. Dreyer
44 Wooden label from tomb of King Aha, Abydos.
   Drawing by Richard Parkinson after W.M.F. Petrie
45 Ebony label with scene of jubilee festival of King Den.
   EA 32650
46 Ivory label recording events of the reign of King Semerkhet.
   EA 32668
47 Statue of King Khasekhemwy.
   Courtesy of the Visitors of the Ashmolean Museum, Oxford
48 Contracted burial in a basketwork coffin.
   EA 52887
49 Funerary enclosure of King Khasekhemwy, Abydos.
   Photo J. Baines
50 Palace-façade brickwork, enclosure of King Khasekhemwy, Abydos.
   Photo Egypt Exploration Society
51 A Late Predynastic tomb at Abydos.
   Photo German Archaeological Institute, Cairo

Index